nut Butter Cookbook for Kids

Judy Ralph and **Ray Gompf**

Illustrated by **Craig Terlson**

Hyperion Books for Children

New York

Text © 1995 by Judy Ralph and Ray Gompf.
Illustrations © 1995 by Craig Terlson. No part of this
book may be used or reproduced in any manner
whatsoever without written permission from the
publisher. Printed in Hong Kong. For information
address Hyperion Books for Children
114 Fifth Avenue, New York, New York, 10011.

A Hyperion Paperback original
First edition: September 1995

1 3 5 7 9 10 8 6 4 2

Library of Congress Cataloging-in-Publication Data
Ralph, Judy.
   The peanut butter cookbook for kids/Judy Ralph
and Ray Gompf; illustrated by Craig Terlson—1st ed.
      p.   cm.
   Includes index.
   ISBN 0-7868-1028-9 (pbk.)—ISBN 0-7868-2110-8
(lib. bdg.)
   1. Cookery (Peanut butter)—Juvenile literature.
[1. Cookery—Peanut butter.]   I. Gompf, Ray.
II. Terlson, Craig, ill.   III. Title.
TX814.5.P38R35   1995
641/6′56596—dc20   94-37852

About this book

This collection of recipes contains great new ways to use peanut butter as well as old favorites that grandma used to make. Each recipe lists all the things you'll need for your baking, and all the ingredients can be found in your kitchen or at your local grocery store. Detailed sketches of each step help make cooking easy, even if you are a beginner. Try a special dish for dinner with family or friends, or make "lollipop" peanut butter cookies as a party activity, or prepare your own peanut butter snack or lunch box treat.

   Depending on the recipe you choose, you may need to use the oven, the microwave, or the heating elements on top of the stove. You may need to use sharp knives, a grater, or the electric mixer. Before you begin, ask an adult for permission and make sure he or she is standing by to assist you when you need help.

When you see this sign in a recipe it signals that you need to get an adult, be alert, and take caution.

Cooking is fun to do, and the best part is eating all the great things you make. Before you start, read the special instructions at the front of the book. Then choose your recipe and begin.

Happy Cooking!

Contents

Peanut butter and your health   4
About the peanut   5
Grow your own peanuts   8
Make your own peanut butter   8
Get ready to bake   9
How to use a microwave   10
How to measure   10
How to crack an egg   10
How to test for doneness   10

Super Snacks   11
PB–Banana Milkshake   12
Peanutty Hot Chocolate   13
Ants on a Log and PB Flowers   14
Cereal Snack   15
Granola Bars   16
Cream Cheese Icing   18
PB Granola   19
PB–Banana Roll-ups   20
Pita Pocket   22
Fruit Roll-ups   23

Hale and Hearty   25
Basic PB Sandwich   26
Fancy PB Sandwich   27
PB Sandwich Variations   27
Quick PB Soup   28
PB Spread/Dip   29
Toasty PB Melt   30
PB Fingers   32
Orange Salad with PB Dressing   34
PB Spicy Chicken and Noodles   36
Peanutty Nachos   38
Easy-As-Pie Pizza   39
Thai Chicken Pizza   42

Chicken Stir-fry with Rice and PB Sauce   45
PB Sauce   47
PB Bran Fake Muffins   49
PB Banana Bread   52

Party Pizazz   54
PB Caramel Corn   55
PB Ice-cream Sundae Rings   57
PB Berry Cone   59
Chocolate PB Sauce   60
PB Pinwheels   61
PB Hockey Puck Sandwiches   63
Traditional PB Cookies   65
Carrot Wagon Wheels   67
PB Banana Cookies   69
Grandpa's Hearty Cookies   71
PB Cookiegram   73
PB Brownies and 3 Icings   76
    Fudge Icing   78
    Peanut/Chocolate Icing   79
    PB Icing   80
PB Butterscotch Beasties   81
Sweet Marie Chocolate Treats   82
Made-in-the-Pan Chocolate Cake with
    PB Icing   84
PB Chocolate Pieces   86
Vanilla PB Squares   87
No-bake PB Cheesecake   89
PB Dessert Pizza   91
PB Honey Pie   92
PB Fudge   94

Measurement Conversion Table   95
Index   96

Peanut butter and your health

Imagine a machine containing pumps, valves, processors, and millions of message-sending and -receiving stations, all working 24 hours a day, 365 days a year, year after year, nonstop. Can you guess what it is? The answer is YOU—your body!

**As the saying goes—
you are what you eat.**

What kind of fuel does it take to keep this machine running smoothly? Sufficient nutrients—foods that contain proteins, carbohydrates, vitamins, minerals, fats, and water—are what the body needs to grow, develop, and be active.

Food guides to healthy eating advise you to choose foods from six different food groups every day from this pyramid. It shows you the importance of eating a variety of foods in the recommended amounts to provide the nourishment you need to keep fit. The three groups at the bottom of the pyramid support the structure and should be the basis of your daily diet. Think of planning meals with fruits, vegetables, and grains and pasta as the main course. These foods give you complex carbohydrates, fiber, and vitamins and minerals.

Peanut butter belongs in the middle of the pyramid with the meat and alternates group. These foods are important too. They contain a lot of protein to make strong muscles, healthy blood, bones, and teeth, and help you grow. Every body cell has protein in it so you need to take in a daily supply. Peanut butter also provides other nutrients such as several B vitamins, vitamin E, minerals such as potassium, calcium, magnesium, phosphorus, zinc, and iron, as well as carbohydrates and fat.

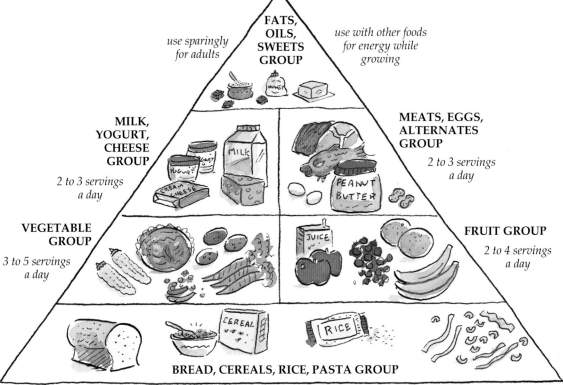

All these nutrients are necessary to help you run, jump, and swim. Peanut butter is a good food choice. It adds variety to your healthy eating plan.

Peanut butter sandwiches or hot dogs make great snacks.

You've probably heard that foods such as peanut butter, eggs, ice cream, cheese, processed meats, and hot dogs have high fat content (fats are shown at the top of the pyramid). As you grow older you'll have to eat these foods in moderation as your parents do. But you're still growing and

Your body takes in food to chew, Then it makes it into you.

need calories from fat for proper growth and development. Fat, like the other five nutrients, is needed by your body every day. For healthy eating it's a good idea to exercise and choose foods that provide other nutrients along with fat. Peanut butter is one of these foods, unlike doughnuts and french fries that provide only small amounts of nutrients but are high in fat, oils, salt, and sugar.

Peanut butter is nourishing. Astronauts in outer space eat space food sticks made from a peanut butter base.

About the peanut

When former President Jimmy Carter moved into the White House, everyone knew that he had been a peanut farmer and had an interest in peanuts. Some of the delegates who nominated him urged, "Make the peanut our national tree." But did you know that peanuts do not grow on trees and they are not nuts either? This plant is a legume related to peas and beans. It could be called a ground pea. A peanut may be called by hundreds of names, including arachide, cacahuete, earth almond, earth cocoa bean, earth nut, goober, grass nut, and ground nut.

The peanut, which we all love to eat, has been around for a long time in many parts of the world, but its origin is 100 percent South American. According to scientists, the peanut evolved thousands of years ago from a wild plant similar to the one we know today. It probably originated in Bolivia (although no one knows for sure) and then spread to other countries.

Molded replicas of peanut pods decorate a water jar found in Peru dated about 1500 B.C.

Molded decorative replicas of peanut pods have been found on ceramic pottery dug from burial sites in Peru, dating to about 1500 B.C. Remains of peanut shells from about 100 B.C. were found in grave sites in Mexico, where peanuts are believed to have been an introduced crop from South America.

Europeans did not know about peanuts until the early 1500s. Explorers and adventurers who visited South America and Mexico took them on their travels as examples of native food crops and were responsible for the peanut's wide distribution. By the late 1500s the peanut

had reached China and the Malay Peninsula. It made its way to Africa when Portuguese slavers brought it from Brazil and planted it on the West Africa coast to provide cheap and nourishing food for their captives.

By the end of the 1600s the holds of slave ships bound for the United States were filled with peanuts—the only food to sustain the slaves on their ocean voyage. Peanuts were grown in the southern states as suitable food only for slaves and animals. But during the American Civil War (1861–1865), soldiers from the North and South who fought in states where peanuts were grown tasted them for the first time and liked them. At the end of the war soldiers returning to the North took peanuts with them. Peanut production increased 200 percent to fill this new demand.

Aztecs, the people who founded the Mexican empire, used a peanut paste similar to peanut butter as a toothache remedy.

Peanuts became very popular as a snack. By the end of the 1800s they were sold fresh roasted in the shell by street vendors and at baseball games and circuses. At this time, about 1890, peanut butter was invented by a physician (his name has not been recorded) in St. Louis as a health food. During the same period in Michigan Dr. John H. Kellogg, famous for corn flakes, gave peanut butter to his patients for easily digested nourishment. In 1903 Ambrose Straub of St. Louis patented a machine to make it.

P. T. Barnum introduced peanuts to New York City at his circus in 1870.

In the early 1900s Amedeo Obici, an Italian immigrant who had settled in Brooklyn, had the idea of selling salted, roasted peanuts without shells which he packaged in see-through bags. The demand was so great he established a large enterprise called the Planters Peanut Company.

Cultivating peanuts was encouraged

A peanut vendor, about 1890.

by George Washington Carver (1864–1943), an African-American botanist, who was anxious to improve southern economy by promoting the use and value of the peanut. He discovered 300 uses for peanuts, peanut shells, and peanut foliage. To demonstrate the peanut's versatility he served an entire meal based on peanuts to a group of Alabama businessmen: peanut soup, peanut "chicken," peanuts prepared as vegetables, peanut flour bread, salad with peanut oil dressing, peanut ice cream, peanut cookies, peanut candy, and "coffee" made from peanuts.

Carver was a pioneer in peanut research. He discovered ways to increase

No part of the peanut is wasted. Even the shells are processed into wallboard, kitty litter, and fireplace logs.

crop yields and encourage the growing of better peanuts. The peanut is now one of the world's leading crop foods. World production is around 20 million tons—enough to encircle the world with a band of peanuts 90 feet wide.

The United States is the third largest producer of peanuts, behind China and India. Although salted, roasted peanuts continue to be an important snack food, the main use of peanuts in North America is to make peanut butter and its most popular use is for sandwiches. Over 700 million pounds of peanut butter—smooth and chunky—are produced annually in the United States.

In India peanuts are used in soups and stews or coated with sugar to eat as a sweet.

Today, the average person in the U.S. eats about 10 pounds of peanuts per year.

Peanuts are greatly prized in the world for their high food value. But peanut butter continues to be favored in North America because it tastes so good.

Someone in North America eats a peanut butter sandwich every five seconds.

A peanut sat on the railroad track,
Its heart was all a-flutter.
Choo-choo train comes round the bend,
Toot, toot! Peanut butter.

7

Grow your own peanuts

It's very easy to grow your own peanuts.

1 Place a few stones in the bottom of a 10-inch pot and fill with potting or garden soil.

2 Make a hole 1 inch deep and put a shelled raw peanut in the hole.

3 Cover with soil, pat down, sprinkle with water, and place the pot in a warm, sunny window.

4 Keep the soil moist and warm—about 65–70°F.

5 In 5 days the seed's root will be 6 inches long in the soil.

6 In 3 more days the sprout will break the surface of the soil. In another 6 days small leaves unfold. Foliage takes 6 to 8 weeks to develop.

7 Then a stalk with yellow flowers appears. A few days later the stalk ("peg") begins to grow downward.

8 The peg goes into the soil about 2 or 3 inches.

The peanut is the only plant that plants its own seed.

9 The tip of the peg develops into a pod and in 40 to 50 days contains mature peanuts. One plant can make several mature pods.

10 At maturity the plants lose some of their green color. This is the time for harvesting.

11 Pull the plant, shake off the dirt, and hang in a warm dry place until dry and brittle (about a week).

12 Remove the pods. Store in a dry place.

To prepare your home-grown peanuts for eating, spread the pods on a cookie sheet and bake in the oven at 350°F for 15 to 20 minutes. Remove the peanuts from the oven. Allow to cool. Shell, salt, if desired, and EAT!

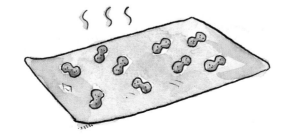

Make your own peanut butter

Put 1 tablespoon of oil (safflower, sunflower, canola, or peanut) in a blender or food processor. Turn the machine on high and add 2 cups of shelled roasted salted peanuts. Process until smooth and creamy (about 20 minutes). Turn the machine off from time to time and scrape down the bowl with a spatula. If you prefer chunky, add pieces of broken peanuts to the mixture at the end of processing. Store the peanut butter in the refrigerator to keep it fresh.

• • • • • • • • • • • •

Natural peanut butter requires re-mixing because the peanut oils rise to the top. Most people prefer blended peanut butter that has no oil on the top. How do the manufacturers do this? Food additives called monoglycerides are used to stabilize the mixture to keep the oil from separating. This peanut butter contains 95 percent peanuts and 5 percent hydrogenated vegetable oil, dextrose, antioxidant, salt, honey, lecithin, whey, and other minor additives. It does not have chemical preservatives or artificial coloring.

Get ready to bake

1 Read the recipe over before you begin. Each recipe has a list of the things you will need. Check to see if you have all the ingredients as well as the proper utensils and baking pans suitable for the recipe.

2 Make sure you have enough cleared counter space to spread out everything you need for baking. Assemble your pans, bowls, spoons, etc., and lay out the recipe book at the desired page.

3 Always wash your hands with soap and water and dry them carefully before you cook or serve. Remember to keep a dish towel handy in case you need to rinse sticky hands while you are baking. Wash your hands if you cough or sneeze.

4 Use a separate spoon for tasting.

5 Wear shoes to protect yourself from spills.

6 Roll up your sleeves while cooking as they can catch on pot handles and cause a spill. Tie back long hair for safety also.

7 If grease catches on fire while you are cooking, smother it with a lid or by throwing baking soda on it.

8 Always use oven mitts to hold or remove a hot pan or dish from the oven or microwave. Set it on a wire cooling rack on the counter. Never put the hot pan directly on the counter. It may burn the surface.

9 When you are cooking on top of the stove remember that liquids become very hot. When liquids bubble constantly they are **boiling**, and boiling liquids can reach a temperature of 425°F. When you are stirring liquids in a saucepan be careful that bursting bubbles do not splash your hands. Always turn saucepan handles so they do not stick out over the stove, to avoid someone bumping them and spilling the hot liquid. Always stir with a long-handled wooden spoon.

10 Sharp knives must be used carefully. Use a breadboard for cutting to protect the counter top. Put knives, grater, and peelers aside after using and wash them separately.

11 Always make sure you have dry hands before you plug in or unplug any appliances such as the electric mixer or the food processor. Do not put your fingers in the bowl or near the moving parts of any appliance when it is running. Use a spatula to scrape the sides of the bowl **only when the machine has been turned off.**

12 Wash and rinse bowls as you finish with them and stack them away from your work area to dry. This keeps your workplace uncluttered, making it easier and safer for food preparation.

13 Always turn the oven or stove burners off when you are not using them. Be sure to leave the stove clean inside and out when you are finished baking.

14 Always rinse uncooked chicken with water before preparing it. Wash your hands and all utensils that have touched the uncooked chicken before continuing with the recipe.

When you see these letters in the recipe it means peanut butter.

How to use a microwave

When a microwave oven is turned on it produces high-frequency radio waves called microwaves. These bounce around on the inside walls of the oven and cause the molecules in the food to move around too. This action causes heat and the heat cooks the food.

MAGNETRON CREATES MICROWAVES

WAVES ARE BOUNCED BY SPINNER

MICROWAVES CAUSE FOOD MOLECULES TO BOUNCE AND COOK.

Safety rules
• Be sure to ask an adult to show you how to use the microwave safely.
• Never turn the microwave on when it is empty.
• Always use oven mitts to lift hot dishes out of the microwave.
• Never open the microwave while it is on.

10

How to measure

MEASURING LIQUID INGREDIENTS
Use a clear glass or plastic liquid measuring cup. Watch the markings on the side to get the correct amount. Check it at eye level to be sure you do not go under or over the mark.

MEASURING DRY INGREDIENTS
Use a set of metal or plastic measuring cups. Fill the container and then use the flat edge of a knife to scrape off the extra amount.

A set of metal or plastic spoons is used for measuring dry or liquid ingredients.

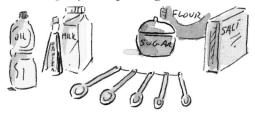

It is important to use exactly what the recipe calls for.

How to crack an egg

1 Set a bowl on the counter.
Hold the egg in one hand and tap it firmly on the rim of the bowl until it cracks.

2 Holding the egg over the bowl, place a thumb on each side of the crack and pull the egg apart. The contents will fall into the bowl.

How to test for doneness

It's easy to tell when muffins or cakes are done. A toothpick prick in the center of one muffin or the cake should come out clean (with no batter on it). Or press your fingertip lightly on the muffin or center of the cake. If done, it will spring back into shape.

PB ~ Banana Milkshake

Makes 4 servings

INGREDIENTS

5 tablespoons smooth
   peanut butter
1 tablespoon honey
3 scoops vanilla ice cream
1 small banana
1 cup cold milk

UTENSILS

Measuring cups and spoons •
Blender • Ice cream scoop
• 4 glasses • Straws

12

1 Put the peanut butter, honey, ice cream, banana, and milk in a blender.

2 Cover and blend on **high** speed for 10 seconds until smooth. Place in a shaker if you want to give it an extra shake.

3 Pour into 4 glasses.

The Shake Song

Sing to the tune of
"Here We Go Round the Mulberry Bush"

This is the way to make a shake,
A quick shake, a healthy shake,
Mixing it up will make it better,
It's very easy to put together.

First put in the peanut butter,
The yummy gooey peanut butter,
And don't forget the honey sweet,
To make your shake the greatest trea

Next step you pour in the milk,
A cup will do, add a banana too,
And ice cream makes it so delicious
Now taste how good this pb shake is

Tips—You can substitute 1/4 cup of chocolate syrup for the banana to make a yummy chocolate shake.

Peanutty Hot Chocolate

Makes 5 cups

INGREDIENTS

3 cups milk

1/3 cup chocolate syrup

2 tablespoons smooth peanut butter

5 large marshmallows

UTENSILS

Measuring cups and spoons •
Medium saucepan
• Wooden spoon • Ladle
• Drinking mugs

1 Put the milk in the saucepan.

2 Turn the stove on to **medium** heat and place the saucepan on the stove. Stir with a wooden spoon until hot but **do not boil**.

3 Stir in the chocolate syrup and the peanut butter. Continue stirring until blended and hot. Turn the heat off.

4 Ladle the hot chocolate into serving mugs. Top with marshmallows.

Tips—Put 1/2 cup of whipping cream in a bowl. Beat with an electric mixer until thick. Place a mound of whipped cream on top of the hot chocolate in the mug. Or add a scoop of ice cream. Delicious!

UTENSILS
Small bowl • Electric mixer

Ants on a Log and PB Flowers

Makes 2 snacks

INGREDIENTS

1 medium apple
1 celery stalk
1/4 cup peanut butter
Raisins

UTENSILS

Paring knife • Breadboard
• Table knife and spoon
• Serving plate

1 Wash and dry the apple.

2 Using a breadboard and paring knife, carefully cut the apple into fourths.

Remove the core with a spoon, then cut each fourth into 4 slices.

3 Wash a celery stalk. Cut it into 2-inch lengths. Fill with soft peanut butter.

4 Place a few raisins on each celery piece to make "ants on a log." Place on the serving plate.

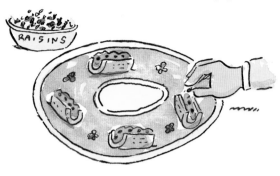

5 Spread peanut butter on one side of the apple pieces.

6 On the same plate place the raisins in a pile in the center. Arrange the apple pieces like flower petals. Serve right away.

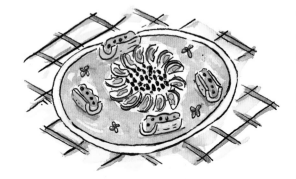

Cereal Snack

Makes 16 squares

INGREDIENTS

1 teaspoon butter, at room
temperature
1 cup puffed wheat
3-1/2 cups corn flakes
1 cup rice crispies
1 cup corn syrup
1/3 cup sugar
1/2 cup peanut butter

UTENSILS

Measuring cups and spoons •
Paper towel • 8" square cake pan
• Large mixing bowl •
Large saucepan • Wooden spoon
• Fork

1 Using the paper towel, spread 1 teaspoon of butter evenly over the bottom and sides of the cake pan.

2 Put the cereals in a mixing bowl and set it aside.

3 Put the corn syrup, sugar, and peanut butter in a saucepan. Turn the stove on to **medium** heat and place the saucepan on the stove.

4 Carefully stir the mixture with a wooden spoon until the mixture bubbles. Turn the heat off.

15

5 Pour the mixture over the cereals. Stir until well mixed.

6 Press the mixture evenly into the pan with your hands or a fork.

7 Place in the refrigerator to harden. Remove for 5 minutes before cutting into squares.

16

Granola Bars

Makes 24 bars

INGREDIENTS

1 cup (2 sticks) plus 2 teaspoons butter, at room temperature
1/4 cup peanut butter
1-1/2 cups firmly packed brown sugar
2 eggs
1/4 cup corn syrup
1 teaspoon vanilla extract
1 tablespoon grated orange peel
1-3/4 cups flour
1/2 cup skim milk powder
1 teaspoon salt
1 teaspoon baking soda
1-1/2 cups rolled oats
3/4 cup shredded coconut
1/3 cup sesame seeds
1/2 cup wheat germ
Cream Cheese Icing (page 18)

UTENSILS

Measuring cups and spoons •
Paper towel • 13" x 9" cake pan
• Large and medium mixing bowls
• Electric mixer • Spatula
• Wooden spoon • Sifter
• Oven mitts • Wire cooling rack

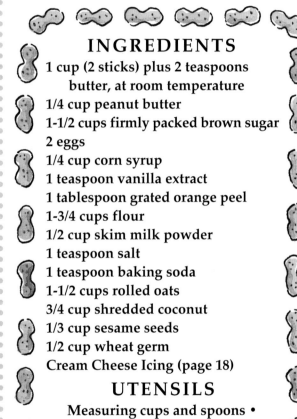

1 Place the oven rack in the center of the oven. Turn on the oven to 350°F.

2 Using the paper towel, spread 2 teaspoons of butter evenly over the bottom and sides of the cake pan.

3 Put the 2 sticks of butter, the peanut butter, and brown sugar in the large mixing bowl. Using the electric mixer on **medium** speed, beat until the mixture is creamy and smooth.

4 Add the eggs, corn syrup, and vanilla. Continue beating until blended.

5 Add the grated orange peel to the creamed mixture and stir well with a wooden spoon.

6 Sift together the flour, skim milk powder, baking soda, and salt into the medium-sized mixing bowl.

7 Add the rolled oats, coconut, sesame seeds, and wheat germ to the flour mixture. Stir with a wooden spoon.

8 Add the dry ingredients to the creamed mixture. Using the electric mixer, beat on **medium** speed until blended.

Stop from time to time to scrape the sides of the bowl with the spatula.

9 Spread the batter into the cake pan, using the spatula.

10 Place the cake pan in the oven and set the timer for 25 to 30 minutes. Test for doneness. A toothpick should come out clean (see page 10).

11 Turn the oven off. Wearing the oven mitts, transfer the pan to the cooling rack for 15 minutes. Then place in the refrigerator to cool.

12 Ice with Cream Cheese Icing. Cut into squares.

Cream Cheese Icing

INGREDIENTS

4 ounces soft cream cheese
1 cup powdered sugar
1 tablespoon butter, at
    room temperature
1 tablespoon milk
1 teaspoon vanilla extract
1/2 cup chocolate chips

UTENSILS

Measuring cups and spoons •
Small mixing bowl
• Electric mixer • Spatula

1 Put the cream cheese, powdered sugar, and butter in the mixing bowl. Using the electric mixer on **low** speed, beat until the mixture is smooth.

2 Add the milk and vanilla and beat until the icing is creamy.

3 Spread the icing on the cooled, uncut bars. Decorate with chocolate chips. Cut and serve.

PB Granola

Makes 10 cups

INGREDIENTS

1 cup peanut butter
2 tablespoons honey
1/4 cup vegetable oil
8 cups assorted dry cereals
2 cups shelled peanuts
1/2 cup sunflower seeds
1/2 cup raisins
1/2 cup carob chips

UTENSILS

Measuring cups and spoons •
Large saucepan • Wooden spoon
• Roasting pan • Oven mitts
• Wire cooling rack

1 Place an oven rack near the center of the oven. Turn on the oven to 325°F.

2 Put the peanut butter, honey, and oil in a large saucepan.

3 Turn the stove on to **low** heat and place the saucepan on the stove. Stir with a wooden spoon until well blended. Turn the heat off.

4 Put the cereals, peanuts, and seeds in the roasting pan. Pour the peanut butter mixture over the cereal mixture. Stir well to combine.

5 Place the pan in the oven. Set the timer for 5 minutes.

6 Wearing the oven mitts, open the oven door and stir the mixture with the wooden spoon. Set the timer for 5 minutes more.

19

7 Wearing the oven mitts, transfer the pan to the wire cooling rack. Turn the oven off.

8 Add the raisins and carob chips. Stir well. Allow to cool.

9 Store in a tightly covered container.

PB~Banana Roll-ups

Makes 3 snack "bites"

INGREDIENTS

1 slice of fresh bread
2 tablespoons peanut butter
1/2 ripe banana

UTENSILS
Measuring spoons • Table knife
• Breadboard • Rolling pin
• Toothpicks

1 Using the table knife and a breadboard, carefully remove the crusts from the slice of bread.

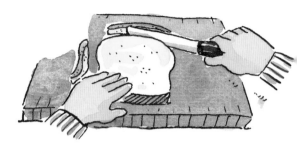

2 Flatten the bread with a rolling pin.

3 Spread the peanut butter on the bread with the table knife.

4 Place the banana at one end of the bread slice. Roll up and secure with toothpicks.

5 Cut with the bread knife into 1-inch pieces or serve as a long log. Be sure to remove toothpicks before eating.

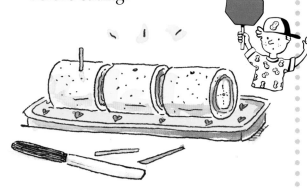

For variety—
On top of the peanut butter sprinkle finely shredded toasted coconut, finely grated chocolate and orange peel, or crunchy granola.

Tips—Save crusts
Put the crusts in a resealable bag or plastic container and freeze until needed for

- **salad croutons** (cut in bite-size pieces, toast in the oven, and toss with salad)

- **bread crumbs** (roll dried crusts between 2 sheets of wax paper—and use for coating meat)

- **stuffing for poultry** (tear in small pieces and freeze until needed)

- **feeding the birds** (tear in small pieces and put in the bird feeder)

- **soup "boats"—fresh** (cut fresh crusts in small pieces) **or toasted** (cut fresh or frozen crusts in pieces, place on a greased cookie sheet, sprinkle with garlic powder, bake in the oven at 350°F for 5 minutes, stir, and continue baking until golden brown)

Can you think of any other uses?

21

Pita Pocket

Makes 1 snack

INGREDIENTS

Whole wheat pocket bread (pita)
2 tablespoons peanut butter
Your choice of the following
fillings:
- **light cream cheese and a dash**
  of spice
- **a few slices of cucumber**
- **mashed banana and cinnamon**
- **cranberry sauce**
- **drained, crushed pineapple**
- **mayonnaise with chopped**
  green onion and lettuce
- **grated carrot and chopped**
  raisins

UTENSILS

Tablespoon • Table knife
• Small dish • Serving dish

1 Cut the pita in half crosswise. (You'll only need one half.) Carefully open the pita pocket with a table knife.

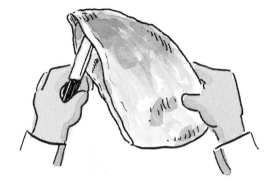

2 Spread 1 tablespoon of peanut butter on each side of the pocket.

3 Prepare one of the fillings in the dish. You may wish to be inventive and make up your own combination.

4 Carefully spoon the filling into the pocket.

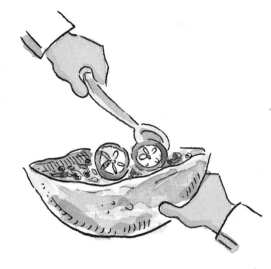

5 Place the finished pita snack on a serving plate.

Great for lunch
boxes too.

Fruit Roll-ups

*Makes 8 medium rolls
or 12 small rolls*

INGREDIENTS

1-3/4 cups unsweetened
applesauce
1/3 cup peanut butter
1 tablespoon honey
1 teaspoon unflavored gelatin

UTENSILS

2 jelly roll pans • Plastic wrap
• Measuring cups and spoons
• Medium mixing bowl •
Electric mixer • Spatula • Lifter
• Oven mitts • Wire cooling rack
• Table knife

1 Place oven racks in the two middle positions of the oven. Turn on the oven to 150°F, or as low a setting as possible.

2 Line the jelly roll pans with plastic wrap. Set aside.

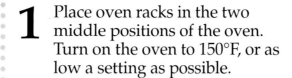

3 Put all the ingredients in the mixing bowl. Using the electric mixer on **medium** speed, blend well.

4 With a spatula, spread the "mushy" mixture as thin and smooth as possible on the lined jelly roll pans. Leave 1 inch around all edges.

Using the edge of the lifter, smooth out any high or low spots.

5 Place the pans in the oven and leave the oven door propped slightly open. Bake 6 hours.

23

The fruit leather is ready when it can be separated from the plastic wrap and the surface is not sticky.

6 Turn the oven off. Wearing the oven mitts, carefully transfer the pans to a cooling rack.

7 While the leather is warm, use the table knife to cut it into 4 or 6 pieces per pan.

8 Roll the leather immediately and wrap in new plastic wrap.

Store the roll-ups in the refrigerator in a resealable plastic bag to protect them from moisture.

Did you know?
Peanut butter is the third great American snack food behind hot dogs and pizza.

Tips—How to set the table

1 Knives are placed to the right of the plate, sharp edge towards the plate. Spoons are placed to the right of the knives, bowls up. Forks are placed to the left of the plate. They are arranged in order of use (depending on your menu), from inside out. All cutlery should be 1 inch from the table edge.

2 Glasses are placed at the tip of the knife.

3 Bread and butter plates are placed to the left of the tip of the fork. Bread and butter knives are placed across the bread and butter plates, sharp edge towards the center of the plate.

4 Napkins are folded and placed to the left of forks with the open corner to the lower right or may be placed on the dinner plate.

5 Foods are served to and removed from the left, using the left hand.

6 Water glasses are filled three-quarters full, just before people sit down to the meal.

7 Beverages are served to and removed from the right, using the right hand.

8 When one course is finished, all food service for that course is removed from the table before serving the next course.

Hale and Hearty

Basic PB Sandwich

Makes 1 sandwich

INGREDIENTS

2 slices bread
2 tablespoons peanut butter

UTENSILS

Measuring spoons • Table knife
• Breadboard • Bread knife •
Fancy cookie cutters

1 Place 2 slices of bread flat on the breadboard.

2 Put 2 tablespoons of peanut butter on one slice of bread. Spread evenly, using the table knife.

3 Place the bread slices together so that the peanut butter is in the middle.

4 Use the bread knife to cut the sandwich in half, quarters, or strips.

Did you know?

A glass of milk, a peanut butter sandwich, and an orange make a balanced meal.

Fancy PB Sandwich

1 Use cookie cutters to create a shape from each slice. Make sure you have 2 of each shape for the sandwich.

Proceed with **Steps 2** and **3** (see page 26).

4 Decorate the sandwich with pieces of vegetables to make faces, etc.

PB Sandwich Variations

1 Begin with **Steps 1** and **2** (see page 26) for Basic PB Sandwich.

3 On the slice of bread that does not have peanut butter, spread another topping. Choose from the ingredients in the picture.

Did you know?

Soda crackers, melba toast, rusks, graham crackers, or potato chips make good "breadless" sandwiches. Spread peanut butter on one side of one cracker. Place another cracker over the top. You can also add jam or jelly or any of the other toppings that you like.

Quick PB Soup

Makes 4 servings

INGREDIENTS

2 celery stalks
1 carrot
1 small onion
2 tablespoons butter
1/2 cup peanut butter
10-ounce can cream of chicken soup
1 soup can of milk
1 soup can of water

UTENSILS

Measuring cups and spoons •
Paring knife • Vegetable peeler
• Breadboard • Large saucepan
• Wooden spoon • Can opener
• Soup ladle • 4 soup bowls

1 Wash the celery and carrot. Peel the onion with the paring knife. Peel the carrot with the vegetable peeler. Using the breadboard and paring knife, cut the vegetables into small pieces.

2 Put the butter and vegetables in the saucepan. Turn the stove on to **medium-low** heat and place the saucepan on the stove.

3 Cook and stir the vegetables with the wooden spoon until they are soft (*do not brown*).

4 Add the peanut butter and stir until mixed.

5 Using the can opener, open the can of soup. Add the soup, milk, and water to the saucepan. Stir well.

6 Turn the heat to **medium**. Cook the soup until it is hot but *do not let it bubble* (boil).

7 Turn the heat off. Ladle the soup into the bowls. Serve with crackers or crusty bread.

PB Spread/Dip

Makes 1 cup

INGREDIENTS

3/4 cup mayonnaise
2 tablespoons peanut butter
1 tablespoon prepared mustard
1/4 teaspoon Worcestershire sauce
1/8 teaspoon garlic powder
Dash of pepper
1 teaspoon chopped chives

UTENSILS

Measuring cups and spoons •
Small mixing bowl
• Mixing spoon • Serving bowl

1 Put all the ingredients in the mixing bowl and stir to mix well.

2 Pour the mixture into the serving bowl and place in the refrigerator to thicken.

3 Use as a spread on sandwiches with bologna or ham, or as a dip for crackers or raw vegetables.

Toasty PB Melt

Makes 2 to 4 servings

INGREDIENTS

2 slices bacon
2 slices bread
2 tablespoons peanut butter
2 slices processed cheese

UTENSILS

Frying pan • Lifter • Paper towel
• Toaster • Cookie sheet
• Measuring spoons • Table knife
• Oven mitts • Wire cooling rack

1 Place the bacon in the frying pan. Turn the stove on to **medium** heat and place the frying pan on the stove. Fry bacon until just crisp. Turn with the lifter to cook both sides.

Wrap the bacon in a paper towel to soak up the extra fat.

2 Toast the bread slices and place them on the cookie sheet.

3 Spread each slice with 1 tablespoon of peanut butter.

4 Put 1 slice of bacon on each slice of toast. Cover each slice with a cheese slice.

5 Place the oven rack near the center of the oven. Turn on the oven to **broil**.

6 Place the cookie sheet in the oven and set the timer for 4 minutes. Cheese should be melted. Turn the oven off.

7 Wearing the oven mitts, transfer the cookie sheet to the cooling rack. Serve immediately.

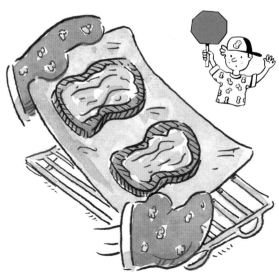

To microwave

1 Arrange the bacon on a microwave-safe dish. Cover with paper towels to prevent grease from splattering. Microwave on **high** power for 3 minutes.

2 Remove from the microwave oven wearing oven mitts. Wrap the bacon in paper towels. Go back to **Steps 2**, **3**, and **4** (see page 30), placing the toasted slices on a microwave-safe dinner plate.

3 Place the plate in the microwave oven and melt the cheese on **high** power for 20 to 30 seconds. Remove plate wearing the oven mitts. Serve immediately.

Variation— Follow Steps 1, 2, and 3 (see page 30). Follow Step 4 but add 1 tomato cut in small pieces on top of the bacon. Sprinkle with 1/4 teaspoon of brown sugar and a pinch of salt and pepper. Cover with cheese. Melt the cheese using the oven or the microwave as described above.

PB Fingers

Makes 6 servings

INGREDIENTS

1 teaspoon butter, at room
   temperature
6 slices of french bread
1 cup crunchy peanut butter
2 eggs
3/4 cup milk
Cracker crumbs

UTENSILS

Measuring cups and spoons •
Paper towel • Cookie sheet
• Breadboard • Bread knife •
Table knife • Large mixing bowl
• Whisk • Wax paper • Slotted
spoon • Lifter • Oven mitts
• Wire cooling rack

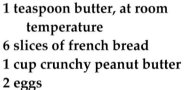

1 Place the oven rack near the center of the oven. Turn on the oven to 400°F.

2 Using the paper towel, spread the butter evenly over the cookie sheet.

3 Using the breadboard and bread knife, slice six 1/2-inch-thick slices of bread.

4 Cut the crusts off the bread slices. Cut the slices in lengthwise strips.

5 Using the table knife, spread the peanut butter on the bread strips.

6 Put the eggs and milk in the mixing bowl. Using the whisk, beat until the mixture is bubbly and frothy.

7 Spread the cracker crumbs on a sheet of wax paper. Using the slotted spoon, dip each strip of bread into the egg mixture and quickly place the strip in the cracker crumbs.

8 Coat both sides of the bread strips. Place the strips on the cookie sheet.

9 Place the cookie sheet in the oven and set the timer for 3 minutes. When ready, the strips should be golden brown. Wearing the oven mitts, slide the oven rack out slightly. Using the lifter, turn the strips and bake 2 more minutes.

10 Turn the oven off. Wearing the oven mitts, transfer the cookie sheet to the cooling rack. Serve immediately.

Did you know? Peanut butter removes gum from hair. Just smear it on the gummed spot. It will pill with the gum and you can pick it off. Then shampoo the hair. You can do this with dogs, too, but if you try it on your cat, omit the shampoo. The cat will lick its own fur.

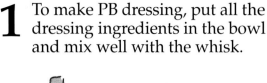

Orange Salad with PB Dressing

INGREDIENTS

— PB DRESSING —
Makes 1 cup

1/2 cup mayonnaise
2 tablespoons honey
2 tablespoons peanut butter
1 tablespoon oil
Pinch of pepper

— SALAD —
Makes 6 servings

1 small head romaine lettuce
2 green onions
2 celery stalks
2 teaspoons sugar
1/4 cup slivered almonds
1 can mandarin orange segments
Bacon bits
Freshly ground pepper

UTENSILS

Measuring cups and spoons •
Mixing bowl • Whisk • Colander
• Paper towels • Salad bowl
• Breadboard • Paring knife
• Small frying pan • Wooden
spoon • Wax paper • Can opener •
Salad tongs•

1 To make PB dressing, put all the dressing ingredients in the bowl and mix well with the whisk.

2 Place in the refrigerator until ready to use.

3 To make the salad, separate and wash the lettuce leaves. Drain in the colander.

4 Pat dry with paper towels. Tear the lettuce into small pieces. Put in the salad bowl.

5 Using the breadboard and paring knife, peel and cut the onions into small pieces. Add to the salad bowl.

6 Wash the celery stalks and cut them in small pieces. Add to the salad bowl.

7 Put the sugar and slivered almonds in the frying pan. Turn the stove on to **medium** heat and place the frying pan on the stove.

8 Stir with the wooden spoon until the sugar melts and coats the almonds. Pour onto wax paper. Set aside until ready to serve.

9 Using the can opener, open the can of oranges and drain off the juice, using the colander. Add the oranges to the salad bowl.

10 Add the almonds and a sprinkling of bacon bits to the salad.

11 Add the PB dressing a little at a time, tossing the salad with the salad tongs (or a large fork and spoon) until the lettuce is lightly moistened.

Sprinkle with more pepper, if desired. Serve immediately.

PB Spicy Chicken and Noodles

Make the dressing the day before you serve the salad.

INGREDIENTS

SPICY DRESSING
Makes 2-1/2 cups dressing

3 garlic cloves, crushed in press
3/4 cup soy sauce
1/3 cup lime juice
3 tablespoons sugar
3 tablespoons peanut butter
1-1/2 cups vegetable oil
1/4 teaspoon ground red pepper

SALAD
Makes 6 servings

1/2 package Chinese noodles or spaghetti
2 cucumbers
3 carrots
1/2 cup shelled roasted peanuts
3 cooked chicken breast halves

UTENSILS

Measuring cups and spoons •
Deep mixing bowl • Whisk
• Garlic press • Large saucepan
• Colander • Serving platter
• Vegetable peeler • Paring knife
• Grater • Rolling pin • Wax paper

1 Make the dressing: Put the garlic, soy sauce, lime juice, sugar, peanut butter, oil, and red pepper in the bowl. Whisk well to blend.

2 Cover the bowl and place it in the refrigerator for 1 day. Remove from the refrigerator just before using.

3 Prepare the noodles as directed on the package.

4 Drain the noodles in the colander. Put the noodles on the serving platter.

5 Wash the cucumbers and carrots. Peel vegetables with the vegetable peeler.

6 Using the breadboard and paring knife, cut the cucumber into small pieces.

7 Using the grater, shred the carrots.

8 Spread the vegetables over the noodles.

9 Using the breadboard and paring knife, cut the chicken into small pieces. Spread them over the cucumbers and carrots.

10 Put the peanuts between 2 sheets of wax paper. Roll with the rolling pin to crush.

11 Sprinkle the crushed nuts over the chicken.

12 Remove the dressing from the refrigerator and pour over the salad. Serve immediately.

Peanutty Nachos

Makes 12 nachos

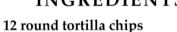

INGREDIENTS

12 round tortilla chips
1 tablespoon peanut butter
5 tablespoons salsa or taco sauce
3/4 cup cheddar cheese
   (or Monterey Jack cheese)

UTENSILS

2 aluminum foil pie plates •
Measuring cups and spoons
• Small mixing bowl • Mixing
spoon • Grater • Oven mitts
• Wire cooling rack

1 Place the oven rack near the center of the oven. Turn on the oven to 400°F.

2 Arrange 6 chips in each foil plate.

3 Put the peanut butter and salsa in the mixing bowl and stir to mix.

4 Put a little of the mixture on each chip.

5 Using the grater, shred the cheese.

38

6 Sprinkle the cheese over the chips.

7 Put the pie plates in the oven. Set the timer for 4 minutes. Turn the oven off.

8 Wearing the oven mitts, transfer the pie plates to the cooling rack. Serve immediately.

Easy-As-Pie Pizza

Makes a 12-inch pizza

INGREDIENTS

— CRUST —

1 teaspoon butter, at room temperature
7 large eggs
1/2 cup flour
1/2 teaspoon salt
1/2 teaspoon oregano

— TOPPING —

1 can (7-1/2 ounces) pizza sauce
2 tablespoons peanut butter
1 small green pepper
1 medium tomato
1 medium onion
1 cup sliced pepperoni
1/2 cup sliced cooked ham, chopped
2 ounces cheddar cheese
4 ounces mozzarella cheese

UTENSILS

Measuring cups and spoons •
12-inch pizza pan • Paper towel
• Blender • Wooden spoon •
Oven mitts • Wire cooling rack •
Small bowl • Spatula •
Breadboard • Paring knife •
Grater • Pizza cutter

1 Place the oven rack near the center of the oven. Turn on the oven to 350°F.

2 Using the paper towel, spread 1 teaspoon of butter evenly over the pizza pan.

3 Put the eggs, flour, salt, and oregano in a blender and mix until smooth.

4 Pour the mixture into the pan. Place the pan in the oven and set the timer for 15 to 20 minutes.

5 Prepare the topping while the pizza crust is baking. Put the sauce and peanut butter in a bowl and stir with the wooden spoon to mix.

6 Wearing the oven mitts, transfer the pizza pan to the cooling rack.

7 Spread the topping on the pizza crust, using a spatula.

8 Wash the pepper and tomato. Peel the onion. Using the bread-board and the paring knife, cut the vegetables into small pieces.

9 Put the meat and vegetables on the pizza crust.

10 Using the breadboard and the grater, grate the cheeses and sprinkle them over the pizza.

11 Return the pizza pan to the oven and set the timer for 10 minutes. Cheese should be melted. Turn the oven off.

12 Wearing the oven mitts, transfer the pizza pan to the cooling rack.

13 With the pizza cutter, cut the pizza into 8 slices. Serve immediately.

What is it?
Clues
- Some people call it a nut but it isn't.
- If it were in a protein race it might come first.
- When it was banned at a baseball park it almost caused a riot.

41

Thai Chicken Pizza

Make the chicken mixture 1 day before you make the pizza.

INGREDIENTS

—CHICKEN MIXTURE—

1 small carrot
1/2 small onion
1 stalk celery
1 clove garlic
1/2 teaspoon ground ginger
1/2 teaspoon grated lime peel
1/8 teaspoon dried red pepper flakes or chili powder
1/4 teaspoon ground coriander
1/2 teaspoon dried parsley
2 teaspoons brown sugar
4 tablespoons soy sauce
4 tablespoons lime juice
2 tablespoons crunchy peanut butter
1 tablespoon peanut oil
2 boneless skinned chicken breast halves (1 cup of cut-up pieces)

UTENSILS

Measuring cups and spoons •
Breadboard • Paring knife
• Garlic press • Ovenproof
casserole dish • Wooden spoon
• Aluminum foil

1 Using the breadboard and paring knife, peel and cut up the carrot and onion in small pieces. Put in the casserole dish.

2 Wash and cut up the celery and put in the casserole. Peel the garlic and press through the garlic press into the casserole.

3 Add the ginger, lime peel, red pepper flakes, coriander, parsley, brown sugar, soy sauce, lime juice, peanut butter, and peanut oil to the casserole. Stir with the wooden spoon.

4 Rinse the chicken with water. Using the breadboard and the paring knife, cut the chicken into small pieces. Wash your hands, the knife, and breadboard after handling raw chicken.

5 Add the chicken pieces to the casserole mixture and stir. Cover the dish with foil. Place in the refrigerator for 1 day.

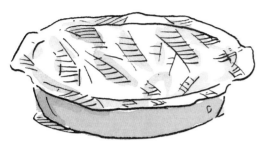

INGREDIENTS
—PIZZA—
Makes a 12-inch pizza

2 teaspoons peanut oil
1 pound frozen bread dough
12 ounces mozzarella cheese
1 carrot
4 green onions
1 cup canned or fresh bean sprouts
1/2 cup shelled roasted peanuts

UTENSILS
Measuring cups and spoons •
Breadboard • Paring knife
• Oven mitts • Wire cooling rack
• 12-inch pizza pan • Paper towel
• Grater • Wax paper • Rolling
pin • Lifter • Pizza cutter

6 One day later remove the casserole dish with the chicken mixture from the refrigerator.

7 Place the oven rack near the center of the oven. Turn on the oven to 325°F. Place the casserole in the oven and set the timer for 20 minutes.

8 Wearing the oven mitts, transfer the casserole to the cooling rack. Allow the chicken mixture to cool.

9 While the chicken mixture cools, start making the pizza. Using a paper towel, spread 2 teaspoons of peanut oil evenly over the pizza pan.

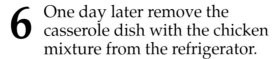

If you prefer thick pizza crust, use the whole 1 pound loaf of dough. If you prefer a thinner crust, cut off 1/3 of the dough, and use only 2/3 of the loaf of dough.

10 Place the thawed bread dough in the pan. Grease your hands. Press the dough with your hands to make it fit the pizza pan.

11 Turn the oven up to 425°F.

12 Using the breadboard and grater, shred the cheese. Put half the cheese on top of the pizza dough, leaving a 1/2-inch border around the edges.

13 Shred the carrot. Using the breadboard and paring knife, trim and wash the green onions and cut them up into fine pieces.

14 Spread the onions, carrot, bean sprouts, and the cooled chicken mixture over the pizza. Top with the remaining cheese.

15 Put the peanuts between 2 sheets of wax paper. Roll with the rolling pin to crush them. Spread over the pizza.

16 Place the pizza pan in the oven. Set the timer for 30 minutes.

17 Turn the oven off. Wearing the oven mitts, transfer the pan to the cooling rack. Cut the pizza into pieces. For spice lovers, serve with warmed PB Sauce (see page 47).

Chicken Stir-fry with Rice and PB Sauce

Makes 4 servings

INGREDIENTS

2 cups raw rice
3 boneless skinned chicken breast
   halves
2 large carrots
2 stalks celery
1 small onion
10-ounce can sliced mushrooms
2 tablespoons vegetable oil
1/2 cup snow peas
1 recipe PB Sauce (page 47)

UTENSILS

Measuring cups and spoons •
Large saucepan • 2 breadboards
• 2 paring knives • Can opener
• Colander • Frying pan • Lifter
• Serving plate

1 Using the large saucepan, prepare four servings of rice according to the directions on the box. Set aside and keep warm.

2 Rinse the chicken with water. Using a breadboard and paring knife, cut the chicken into small pieces. Wash your hands, the knife, and the breadboard after handling raw chicken.

3 Wash the carrots and celery. Using the other breadboard and a clean knife, peel the carrots and onion and cut the carrots, celery, and onion into small pieces.

4 Open the can of mushrooms with the can opener and drain the juice by pouring into the colander.

5 Put the oil in the frying pan. Turn the stove on to **high** heat and place the frying pan on the stove. Add the chicken pieces and stir with the lifter for 2 minutes until browned.

6 Transfer the chicken to a plate and set aside.

7 Put the carrots, onion, and celery in the frying pan and stir with the lifter for 3 minutes.

8 Add more oil if necessary. Add the mushrooms and stir for 1 minute.

9 Return the chicken to the frying pan along with the snow peas. Add the PB Sauce. Cover and cook for 3 to 4 minutes until the chicken is no longer pink inside.

10 Put the hot rice on the serving plate and cover with the chicken stir-fry. Serve immediately.

Did you know? Giving your pet a pill is easy if you disguise it in a lump of peanut butter.

PB Sauce

Makes 2 cups

INGREDIENTS

1 small onion
2 cloves garlic
1 tablespoon cooking oil
1/8 teaspoon hot pepper sauce
1/2 cup peanut butter
2 tablespoons lime juice
2 tablespoons soy sauce
1/2 teaspoon grated fresh ginger root
2 tablespoons milk
2 cups water

UTENSILS

Measuring cups and spoons •
Breadboard • Paring knife
• Garlic press • Grater • Large
saucepan • Wooden spoon • Wire
cooling rack • Covered container

1 Using the breadboard and paring knife, peel the onion and cut it in small pieces.

2 Peel the garlic cloves and put them in the garlic press. Press the garlic into the saucepan.

Add the oil, onion, and pepper sauce.

3 Turn the stove on to **medium** heat and place the saucepan on the stove. Stir the mixture with the wooden spoon until the vegetables are soft and light brown.

4 Add the peanut butter, lime juice, soy sauce, ginger, milk, and water. Continue to stir and cook over **medium** heat until the mixture is smooth and thickened.

47

5 Add more water if the sauce is too thick. Turn the heat off.

6 Transfer the saucepan to the wire rack and let it cool. Store cooled sauce in a covered container in the refrigerator.

Tips— PB Sauce has a variety of uses.
- **With noodles.** Prepare noodles according to the instructions on the box. Put them in a serving dish. Pour the hot sauce over the noodles, and serve immediately.
- **As a sauce for fondue dipping.** Use small pieces of cooked chicken, beef, or pork.
- **Pour hot sauce over a steamed vegetable platter.** Serve immediately.
- **As a sauce for a chicken stir-fry** (see page 45).

PB Bran Fake Muffins

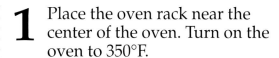

Makes 12 muffins

INGREDIENTS

1/2 cup (1 stick) plus 1 tablespoon
   butter, at room temperature
1/4 cup peanut butter
1 cup firmly packed brown sugar
1-1/3 cups flour
2 teaspoons baking powder
1/4 teaspoon salt
3/4 cup bran
1/2 cup shelled roasted peanuts
1/2 cup raisins
1 cup milk with 2 teaspoons
   lemon juice to sour milk
1 egg, beaten
1 teaspoon baking soda

UTENSILS

Measuring cups and spoons •
Paper towel • Muffin pan
• Large and medium mixing bowls
• Electric mixer • Wax paper
• Rolling pin • Wooden spoon
• Large (2-cup) measuring cup
• Oven mitts • Spatula
• Wire cooling rack

1 Place the oven rack near the center of the oven. Turn on the oven to 350°F.

2 Using a paper towel, spread 1 tablespoon of butter evenly over the bottom and sides of the muffin cups.

3 Put the stick of butter, the peanut butter, and brown sugar in the large mixing bowl. Using the electric mixer on **high** speed, beat until the mixture is light and fluffy.

4 Place the peanuts between 2 sheets of wax paper and crush with a rolling pin. Using the wooden spoon, mix the flour, baking powder, salt, bran, crushed nuts, and raisins together in the medium mixing bowl. Set aside.

5 Put the soured milk, beaten egg, and baking soda in the large measuring cup. Stir until blended.

49

6 Add **half** the flour mixture to the creamed butter mixture. Using the electric mixer on **low** speed, beat until smooth.

7 Stop the mixer, pour in **half** the milk and egg mixture, and mix again. Stop from time to time to scrape the sides of the bowl with the spatula.

Repeat with the remaining flour and then the liquid mixture, mixing **until just blended**. Do not overmix.

8 Fill the cups of the muffin pan 2/3 full. Place the pan in the oven.

9 Set the timer for 15 to 20 minutes. Bake until the muffins are golden brown. Test for doneness (see page 10). Turn the oven off.

10 Wearing the oven mitts, transfer the muffin pan to the cooling rack. Cool for 5 minutes. Turn the pan upside down on the cooling rack to remove the muffins.

Did you know? If you overmix the muffin batter the muffins will be tough and full of tunnels. Muffins should be round on top and straight on the sides. If the oven temperature is too low or too high the muffins will be out-of-shape.

GOOD   OVER MIXED   TUNNELS

When making real muffins, ingredients are not blended with an electric mixer but are combined lightly with a spoon.

Tips—Make a surprise meal-in-a-muffin.

When you have completed **Step 8** and spooned the muffin mixture into a 12-cup muffin pan, place 1 washed small egg on top of some muffins. Continue baking in the same way. When the muffins are done the eggs will be cooked too.

These little meals are so portable and fun to eat. Write a name on the egg or a special message before baking and pack this treat in your lunch box.

Did you know?

- Easy-to-eat, non-messy foods are easiest to pack in the lunch box. Remember a napkin.

- For health reasons, be sure to keep hot foods hot and cold foods cold.
- Freeze food such as cookies, sandwiches, muffins, yogurt, or juice packed in the lunch box and they will be thawed and ready to eat by lunch time while keeping the rest of the lunch cold and safe to eat.
- Soups, stews, and chili add variety to regular bagged lunches. They should be boiling hot when poured into the lunch box thermos.
- Pre-chill the thermos with cold water before adding cold food or liquid.

- Wrap each food separately or use reusable plastic containers to prevent mingling of flavors.

- Individual-sized cans of juice or cartons of milk are handy for the lunch box. Read all packaged food labels to make nutritious choices.

- Canned meat and poultry opened and eaten immediately are great for lunches.

- Fruits and vegetables should be washed before packing in a lunch.
- Don't forget surprises. A note or favorite treat is fun to open.

PB Banana Bread

Makes 3 round loaves

INGREDIENTS

1/3 cup (5-1/3 tablespoons) plus 2
    tablespoons butter, at room
    temperature
2 ripe bananas
2/3 cup white sugar
1/4 cup peanut butter
2 eggs
1-1/2 cups flour
2 teaspoons baking powder
1/4 teaspoon baking soda
2 teaspoons cinnamon
2 tablespoons brown sugar

UTENSILS

Measuring cups and spoons •
Three 10-ounce cans (clean empty
soup cans, tops removed)
• Paper towel • Large, medium,
small mixing bowls • Fork
• Electric mixer • Spatula • Sifter
• Teaspoon • Oven mitts
• Wire cooling rack

1 Place the oven rack near the center of the oven. Turn on the oven to 350°F.

2 Using the paper towel, spread 2 tablespoons of butter evenly inside the 3 cans, over the sides and bottoms.

3 Put the bananas in the large mixing bowl. Mash with a fork. Add the 1/3 cup butter, the white sugar, and peanut butter. Using the electric mixer on **medium-high** speed, beat the mixture for 2 minutes.

4 Add the eggs and beat again until thoroughly mixed.

5 Sift the flour, baking powder, and baking soda into the medium mixing bowl.

6 Add the flour mixture, a little at a time, to the banana mixture. Using the electric mixer on **medium** speed, beat until well blended. The batter will be thick.

7 Divide the batter among the three cans, using the spatula to scrape the bowl. Fill cans 2/3 full.

8 Put the cinnamon and brown sugar in the small mixing bowl. Mix with a spoon and sprinkle on top of each can.

9 Place the cans in the oven. Set the timer for 35 to 40 minutes. Test for doneness (see page 10).

10 Turn off the oven. Wearing the oven mitts, transfer the cans to the cooling rack. Cool bread for 7 minutes. Turn the cans upside down to remove the bread. Cool completely before slicing.

Tips—If you prefer to have a loaf of PB Banana Bread, pour the batter into a greased 9" x 5" x 3" loaf pan and sprinkle the sugar mixture on top. Bake for 1 hour.

Did you know?

A minister of trade in England wanted to promote peanuts. He had a suit made from peanut husk fiber. But the suit fell apart in a few days because it could not withstand the wear and the damp weather.

PB Caramel Corn

Makes 2 large bowls

INGREDIENTS

Large bowl of *popped* popcorn
1/4 cup (1/2 stick) butter
1 cup firmly packed brown sugar
1/4 cup corn syrup
2 tablespoons peanut butter
1/2 teaspoon baking soda
1/2 teaspoon vanilla extract

UTENSILS

Measuring cups and spoons •
Large roasting pan • Large saucepan
• Wooden spoon • Wire cooling rack
• Oven mitts • 2 large serving bowls

1 Place the oven rack near the center of the oven and turn on the oven to 250°F.

2 Put the popped corn in a large roasting pan.

3 Put the butter in the large saucepan. Turn the stove on to **medium** heat and place the saucepan on the stove.

Stir with the wooden spoon until the butter is melted.

4 Stir in the brown sugar, corn syrup, and peanut butter. Stir with the wooden spoon until the mixture bubbles (boils).

5 Turn the heat to **low**. Continue boiling (mixture bubbles constantly) and stirring for 5 minutes. Turn the heat off. Transfer the saucepan to the cooling rack.

55

6 Stir in the baking soda and the vanilla. Pour the mixture over the popcorn in the large roasting pan. Add peanuts.

7 Place the pan in the oven and set the timer for 1 hour. Wearing oven mitts, stir every 15 minutes. Turn the oven off.

8 Wearing the oven mitts, transfer the roasting pan to the cooling rack. Cool completely.

9 Break the caramel corn apart and serve in the large bowls.

Easy Microwave Method

1 Put the butter, brown sugar, corn syrup, and peanut butter in a microwave-safe bowl.

2 Microwave on **high** power for 2 minutes. Stop the microwave from time to time to stir the mixture. Repeat until the mixture bubbles (boils).

3 Remove from the microwave. Add baking soda and vanilla and stir with a wooden spoon.

4 Put the **popped** popcorn and peanuts in a large paper bag.

5 Pour on the sauce and close the bag. Microwave on **high** power for 1-1/2 minutes.

6 Remove from the microwave and shake the bag for 1 minute. Open the bag carefully to let hot steam escape. Serve in the large bowls.

PB Ice-cream Sundae Rings

Makes 5 rings

INGREDIENTS

2 tablespoons corn syrup
2 tablespoons butter
1/4 cup mini-marshmallows
1/4 cup crunchy peanut butter
1/2 teaspoon vanilla extract
2 cups rice crispies
1/4 cup shredded coconut
1 quart vanilla ice cream
Chocolate PB Sauce (page 60) or
    decorate with cherries, raisins,
    coconut, colored candies,
    chocolate chips, chocolate wafers,
    licorice, or sparkles

UTENSILS

Measuring cups and spoons •
Large saucepan • Wooden spoon
• Wire cooling rack • Wax paper
• Cookie sheet • Lifter •
Ice cream scoop • 5 serving plates

1 Put the corn syrup, butter, marshmallows, and peanut butter in the saucepan. Turn the stove on to **low** heat. Place the saucepan on the stove.

2 Stir with the wooden spoon until the mixture is melted and smooth. Turn the heat off.

3 Transfer the saucepan to the cooling rack.

4 Add the vanilla, cereal, and coconut and stir until well coated. Cool slightly.

5 Put wax paper on the cookie sheet.

6 Take a small amount of dough for each ring. Use your hands to shape a ring about 3 inches in diameter. Place the ring on the wax-paper-lined cookie sheet.

Make a total of 5 rings. Cover until serving time.

7 Use the lifter to put one ring on each serving plate. Fill the center hole with a scoop of ice cream.

8 Serve with Chocolate PB Sauce or decorate ice-cream "faces" with colored candy eyes, licorice eyebrows, cherry nose, raisin mouth, coconut whiskers, chocolate wafer ears, or sparkles for hair. If you wish, make sundaes in advance and freeze until needed.

Did you know? Ice cream's high energy content (calories) comes from sugar and fat. But it contains small amounts of protein and calcium as well. It's a tasty snack for kids.

PB Berry Cone

Makes 1 cone

INGREDIENTS

1/2 cup fresh fruit pieces (choose from grapes, pears, apples, kiwi, oranges, strawberries, raspberries, blueberries, or melon)
Large ice-cream cone
Chocolate PB Sauce (page 60)
2 scoops of vanilla ice cream

UTENSILS

Breadboard • Paring knife
• Measuring cup • Drinking glass
• Ice-cream scoop

1 Wash and dry the selected fresh fruit. Using the breadboard and the paring knife, cut up any large fruit and set aside.

2 Dip the top of the ice-cream cone in warm Chocolate PB Sauce.

3 Set the cone in the drinking glass. The sauce will harden. Place in the refrigerator until serving time.

4 Add 2 scoops of soft vanilla ice cream. Sprinkle the fruit on top. Drizzle with more Chocolate PB Sauce.

Chocolate PB Sauce

Makes 2 cups

INGREDIENTS

3/4 cup semi-sweet chocolate chips
1/2 cup corn syrup
1/4 cup water
1 teaspoon vanilla extract
1/2 cup peanut butter
2 tablespoons butter

UTENSILS

Measuring cups and spoons •
Medium saucepan
• Wooden spoon

1 Put the chocolate chips, syrup, and water in the saucepan. Turn the stove on to **medium** heat and place the saucepan on the stove.

2 Stir with the wooden spoon until the chocolate is melted and the mixture bubbles (boils). Cook the mixture for 2 minutes, **stirring constantly** so the sauce does not burn.

3 Turn the heat off. Transfer the saucepan to the cooling rack.

4 Add the vanilla, peanut butter, and butter and stir to blend. Cool slightly. Serve. Store unused sauce in a covered container in the refrigerator.

Tips—To reheat the sauce

Put the sauce in a microwave-safe bowl. Place the bowl in the microwave on **medium** power for 1 minute. Stir with a wooden spoon to blend. Repeat until the sauce is smooth and melted.

Or

Put the sauce in a small saucepan. Turn the stove on to **low** heat and place the saucepan on the stove. **Stir constantly** with a wooden spoon until the sauce is smooth and melted.

PB Pinwheels

Makes 35 cookies

INGREDIENTS

3/4 cup corn syrup
3/4 cup white sugar
2 tablespoons butter
3/4 cup peanut butter
4-1/2 cups rice crispies
— ICING —
1/3 cup (5-1/3 tablespoons) butter
2 tablespoons milk
1-1/2 cups powdered sugar
2/3 cup unsweetened cocoa powder

UTENSILS

Jelly roll pan • Wax paper •
Measuring cups and spoons •
• 1 large, 1 medium saucepan
• Wooden spoon • Spatula • Wire
cooling rack • Sifter • Sharp knife

1 Line the jelly roll pan with wax paper.

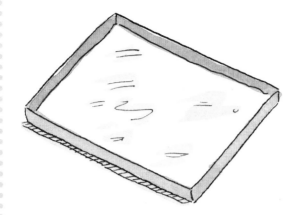

2 Put the corn syrup, sugar, and 2 tablespoons of butter in the large saucepan. Turn the stove on to **medium** heat and place the saucepan on the stove. Stir with the wooden spoon until the sugar dissolves and the mixture bubbles (boils).

3 Turn the heat off. Transfer the saucepan to the cooling rack. Add the peanut butter and stir until blended.

Add the cereal and stir until blended.

4 Using the spatula, scrape the mixture onto the jelly roll pan and spread it evenly with your fingertips or the spatula. Allow to cool.

61

5 To make the icing, put 1/3 cup of butter and the milk in the medium saucepan. Turn the stove on to **low** heat and stir with the wooden spoon until the mixture is melted and blended.

6 Turn the heat off. Transfer the saucepan to the cooling rack. Sift the powdered sugar and cocoa onto the mixture in the saucepan.

Stir with the wooden spoon until the mixture is creamy and blended.

7 Pour the icing mixture over the rice crispy base and spread it evenly with a spatula.

8 Starting from a short end, roll up the mixture, using the wax paper to guide and form a log.

9 Place the log in the refrigerator until it is firm.

10 Cut into 1/2-inch slices with a sharp knife.

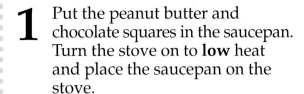

PB Hockey Puck Sandwiches

Makes 18 sandwich cookies

INGREDIENTS

3 tablespoons peanut butter
4 squares semi-sweet chocolate
1 envelope whipped topping
    mix (needs 1/2 cup milk
    and 1/2 teaspoon vanilla
    extract)
36 cookies (chocolate chip or
    peanut butter chip)

UTENSILS

**Measuring cups and spoons •
Medium saucepan
• Wooden spoon • Wire
cooling rack • Cookie sheet**

1 Put the peanut butter and chocolate squares in the saucepan. Turn the stove on to **low** heat and place the saucepan on the stove.

Stir with the wooden spoon until the mixture is melted and smooth. Turn the heat off.

2 Transfer the saucepan to the cooling rack. Allow the mixture to cool.

3 Prepare the whipped topping according to the directions on the envelope.

4 Stir the prepared whipped topping into the chocolate mixture in the saucepan.

5 Arrange 18 cookies on the cookie sheet. Put 1 heaping tablespoon of the chocolate mixture onto each cookie.

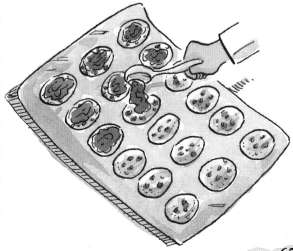

6 Place the other 18 cookies on top, forming cookie sandwiches. The chocolate filling will spread between the cookies.

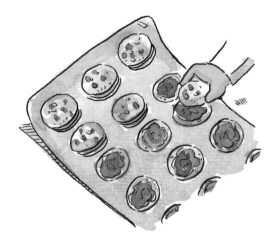

7 Place the cookie sandwiches in the refrigerator until firm (about 3 hours) or freeze cookie sandwiches for later eating.

Did you know?
People in the United States and Canada eat enough peanut butter every year to cover the bottom of the Grand Canyon.

Traditional PB Cookies

Makes 24 cookies

INGREDIENTS

1/2 cup peanut butter
1 cup shortening
1/2 cup white sugar
1/2 cup plus 1/3 cup firmly
    packed brown sugar
1 large egg
1 teaspoon vanilla extract
1 cup flour
1/2 teaspoon salt
1 teaspoon baking soda
1 teaspoon cinnamon

UTENSILS

Measuring cups and spoons •
Cookie sheet • Large and small
mixing bowls • Electric mixer
• Spatula • Wooden spoon
• Small dish • Fork
• Oven mitts • Wire cooling rack

1 Place the oven rack near the center of the oven. Turn on the oven to 350°F.

2 Put the peanut butter, shortening, the white sugar, and 1/2 cup of the brown sugar in the large mixing bowl. Using the electric mixer on **medium** speed, blend until the mixture is creamy.

3 Add the egg and vanilla to the creamed sugar mixture and beat until well blended.

4 In a small bowl stir the flour, salt, and baking soda with a wooden spoon.

Add to the creamed mixture a little at a time. Blend well, using the electric mixer on **low** speed.

Stop from time to time to scrape the sides of the bowl with the spatula.

65

5 Using a teaspoon of dough for each cookie, shape the dough into balls with your hands.

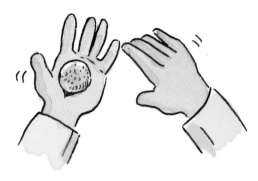

6 Mix the cinnamon and the remaining 1/3 cup of brown sugar in a small dish. Roll the balls in the mixture.

7 Place the balls 1 inch apart on the cookie sheet. Flatten the balls with a fork dipped in the sugar mixture.

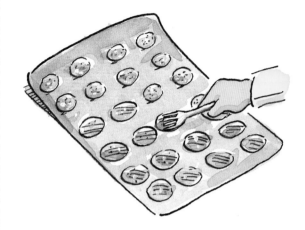

8 Put the cookie sheet into the oven. Set the timer for 8 to 10 minutes. Bake until the cookies are golden brown.

9 Turn the oven off. Wearing the oven mitts, transfer the cookie sheet to the cooling rack.

Let the cookies cool 1 minute before removing with the lifter.

Did you know?

Making "Lollipop" cookies is a great activity for birthday parties. Follow the cookie recipe (page 65). Roll the dough with your hands into 1–1/2–inch balls. Insert a popsicle stick into the ball. Then lay the balls on the cookie sheet (10 to 13 balls per cookie sheet). Dip a flat-bottomed glass in sugar and flatten the cookies. Decorate with raisins, chocolate chips, snipped dried fruit, colored candies, sliced gumdrops. Bake in the oven (375°F) for 8 to 10 minutes. Transfer the cookie sheet to the cooling rack. Immediately lift the cookies with the lifter to a flat surface. Push the stick farther into the cookie. Cool completely. Your lollipop-on-a-stick cookie is ready for eating.

Carrot Wagon Wheels

Makes 36 cookies

INGREDIENTS

1/2 cup peanut butter
1/2 cup shortening
1/2 cup firmly packed brown sugar
1/4 cup white sugar
1 egg
1 teaspoon vanilla extract
1 cup flour
1 teaspoon salt
1 teaspoon baking soda
1 cup bran cereal
1/2 cup shelled roasted peanuts
1 cup shredded carrots (page 68)

UTENSILS

Measuring cups and spoons •
Large and medium mixing bowls
• Electric mixer • Wax paper
• Rolling pin • Wooden spoon
• Cookie sheet • Fork • Oven mitts
• Wire cooling rack • Lifter

1 Place the oven rack near the center of the oven. Turn on the oven to 350°F.

2 Put the peanut butter, shortening, and sugars in the large mixing bowl. Using the electric mixer on **medium** speed, blend until the mixture is creamy.

3 Add the egg and vanilla to the creamed sugar mixture and beat until light and fluffy.

4 In a medium bowl, mix the flour, salt, baking soda, and cereal with a wooden spoon.

5 Add the flour mixture to the creamed mixture and beat on **medium** speed until smooth.

Place the peanuts between 2 sheets of wax paper and, using the rolling pin, crush them.

6 Stir the carrots and peanuts into the cookie dough.

7 Using a teaspoon of dough for each cookie, shape the dough into balls with your hands.

8 Place the balls 1 inch apart on the cookie sheet. Flatten the balls with a fork.

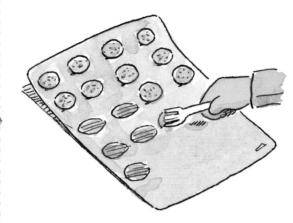

9 Place the cookie sheet in the oven. Set the timer for 10 to 12 minutes. Bake until the cookies are lightly browned around the edges. Turn the oven off.

10 Wearing the oven mitts, transfer the cookie sheet to the cooling rack. Let the cookies cool 3 minutes before removing with the lifter.

Tips—How to shred carrots: Wash and peel 2 large carrots. Cut off the ends. Shred with a grater or in a food processor. Measure 1 cup.

PB Banana Cookies

Makes 48 cookies

INGREDIENTS

1/2 cup (1 stick) butter, at room
    temperature
1/2 cup peanut butter
1 cup plus 1/4 cup sugar
1 ripe banana
1 egg
1 teaspoon vanilla extract
1-1/2 cups flour
1/2 teaspoon baking powder
1-1/2 cups rolled oats
1 tablespoon cinnamon

UTENSILS

Measuring cups and spoons •
Large mixing bowl
• Electric mixer • Sifter • Spatula
• Wooden spoon • Plastic wrap
• Cookie sheet • Small dish
• Fork • Oven mitts
• Wire cooling rack • Lifter

1 Place the oven rack near the center of the oven. Turn on the oven to 375°F.

2 Put the butter, peanut butter, and 1 cup of the sugar in the large mixing bowl. Using the electric mixer on **medium** speed, beat until smooth and creamy.

3 Mash the banana with a fork. Add it with the egg and vanilla and beat until the mixture is light and fluffy.

4 Sift the flour and baking powder into the creamed mixture, a little at a time. Blend well, using the electric mixer on **low** speed.

Stop from time to time to scrape the sides of the bowl with the spatula.

5 Stir in the rolled oats with the wooden spoon.

6 Place plastic wrap on top of the bowl and chill in the refrigerator for 30 minutes.

7 Using a teaspoon of dough for each cookie, shape the dough into balls with your hands.

Place the balls 1 inch apart on the cookie sheet to make the first batch.

8 In a small dish, mix together the cinnamon and the remaining 1/4 cup of sugar. Flatten the balls to 1/4 inch thickness with a fork dipped in the mixture.

9 Place the cookie sheet in the oven. Set the timer for 10 to 12 minutes. Bake until golden brown.

10 Wearing the oven mitts, transfer the cookie sheet to the cooling rack. Let the cookies cool 1 minute before removing them with the lifter.

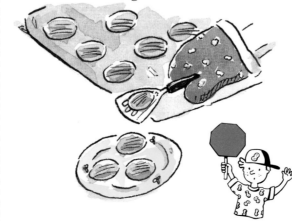

11 Repeat **Steps 7** to **10**, baking one batch at a time, until all the dough is used up.

Modeling dough you can eat

Put 1/2 cup (1 stick) of butter, at room temperature, and 1 cup of sugar in a mixing bowl. Beat at **medium** speed with the electric mixer. Add an egg and beat again. Using a wooden spoon, mix in 2-1/2 cups of flour. Add 1 teaspoon of vanilla and food coloring of your choice. Mix well. Shape into model figures with your hands. Place on a cookie sheet lined with wax paper. Bake in the oven (350°F) for 15 minutes (longer if figures are more than 1/2 inch thick).

Grandpa's Hearty Cookies

Makes 36 cookies

INGREDIENTS

1/2 cup (1 stick) butter, at room temperature
3/4 cup white sugar
2/3 cup firmly packed brown sugar
1-1/2 cups peanut butter
2 eggs
1-1/2 teaspoons vanilla extract
3/4 cup flour
1 cup rolled oats
1/4 cup bran or wheat germ
1/4 cup crushed corn flakes
1/2 teaspoon baking soda
1 cup raisins
1/4 cup shredded coconut

UTENSILS

Measuring cups and spoons •
Large and small mixing bowls
• Electric mixer • Wooden spoon
• Spatula • Cookie sheet • Fork
• Oven mitts • Wire cooling rack
• Lifter

1 Place the oven rack near the center of the oven. Turn on the oven to 350°F.

2 Put the butter, white and brown sugars, and peanut butter in the large mixing bowl. Using the electric mixer on **medium** speed, beat the mixture until smooth and creamy.

3 Add the eggs and vanilla and beat again.

4 Put the flour, oats, bran **or** wheat germ, crushed corn flakes, and baking soda in the small mixing bowl. Stir with the wooden spoon to mix.

5 Add the flour mixture to the creamed mixture, a little at a time. Using the electric mixer on **low** speed, blend together.

Stop from time to time to scrape the sides of the bowl with the spatula.

6 Using the wooden spoon, stir in the raisins and coconut.

7 Using a teaspoon of dough for each cookie, shape the dough into balls with your hands.

8 Place the balls 2 inches apart on the cookie sheet. Flatten the balls with a fork.

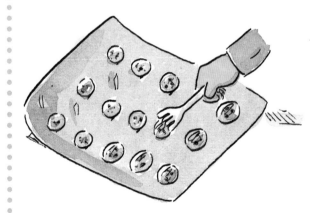

9 Place the cookie sheet in the oven and set the timer for 10 to 12 minutes. Bake until the edges are golden brown.

10 Wearing the oven mitts, transfer the cookie sheet to the cooling rack. Let the cookies cool for 1 minute before removing with the lifter.

11 Repeat, baking one batch of cookies at a time, until all the dough is used.

Tips—You can substitute 1 cup of chocolate chips for the raisins for a super chocolate taste.

PB Cookiegram

Makes 4 cookiegrams

INGREDIENTS

1 cup (2 sticks) plus 2 teaspoons
    butter, at room temperature
1-1/2 cups peanut butter
1 cup firmly packed brown sugar
1/2 cup white sugar
2 eggs
1 teaspoon vanilla extract
2 cups flour
2 teaspoons baking soda
Decorate with colored candies, jelly
    beans, licorice candies, nuts,
    coconut, sprinkles, colored PB
    Icing (page 80)

UTENSILS

Measuring cups and spoons •
Paper towel • Two 8" square cake
pans • Large, medium, small mixing
bowls• Electric mixer • Spatula
    • Sifter • Fork • Plastic wrap
    • Large plate • Oven mitts
    • Wire cooling rack • Lifter

1 Place the oven rack near the center of the oven. Turn on the oven to 350°F.

2 Using the paper towel, spread 1 teaspoon of butter evenly over the bottom and sides of each cake pan.

3 Put the 2 sticks of butter, the peanut butter, and sugars in the large mixing bowl.

4 Using the electric mixer on **medium** speed, beat the mixture until it is light and fluffy.

Stop from time to time to scrape the sides of the bowl with the spatula.

5 Add the eggs and vanilla to the creamed mixture and beat again.

6 Sift together the flour and baking soda into the medium bowl.

7 Add the flour mixture to the creamed mixture and blend on **low** speed until smooth.

Put plastic wrap over the bowl and refrigerate for 1 hour.

8 Put 1/4 of the batter in one cake pan and spread it evenly with your fingertips or a spoon to 1/2 inch from the sides of the pan. Repeat for the second pan.

9 Place the pans in the oven and set the timer for 15 minutes. Bake until golden brown around the edges.

10 Wearing the oven mitts, transfer the pans to the cooling rack. Cool 5 minutes.

11 Bang each pan once on the countertop.

Turn the pans upside down over a plate.

12 Bake the other 2 cookiegrams. Turn the oven off.

13 Decorate each cookiegram with a special message or design.

Tips—For variety, stir in 1/2 cup raisins, chocolate chips, crushed peanuts, or cereal to the dough at the end of Step 7.

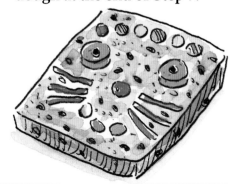

A cookiegram is ideal for a "thank you" for treat bags for birthday party guests.

75

PB Brownies and 3 Icings

Makes 16 squares

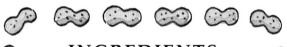

INGREDIENTS

1/3 cup (5-1/3 tablespoons) plus 1
  teaspoon butter, at room
  temperature
2 squares (2 ounces) unsweetened
  chocolate
2 eggs
1 cup plus 1/4 cup sugar
1/2 teaspoon vanilla extract
2/3 cup flour
1/2 teaspoon baking powder
1/2 cup peanut butter
1/2 cup milk

UTENSILS

Measuring cups and spoons •
Paper towel • 8" square cake pan
• Large saucepan • Wooden spoon
• Large, medium, and small mixing
bowls • Wire cooling rack
• Electric mixer • Spatula • Sifter
• Table knife • Oven mitts

1 Place the oven rack near the center of the oven. Turn on the oven to 350°F.

2 Using the paper towel, spread 1 teaspoon of butter evenly on the bottom and sides of the cake pan.

3 Put the chocolate squares and 1/3 cup of butter in the saucepan. Turn the stove on to **low** heat and place the saucepan on the stove.

4 Stir with the wooden spoon until the mixture is melted. Turn the heat off. Place the saucepan on the cooling rack.

5 Put the eggs, 1 cup of the sugar, and the vanilla in the large mixing bowl. Using the electric mixer on **high** speed, blend until the mixture is light and fluffy.

6 Add the melted chocolate to the creamed mixture and blend well on **medium** speed.

7 Pour the mixture into the cake pan using the spatula to scrape the bowl.

8 Sift the flour and baking powder together in the small bowl.

9 Put the peanut butter in the medium bowl. Using the electric mixer on **low** speed, beat 1/4 cup of sugar and the milk with the peanut butter until blended.

10 Add the flour mixture and continue blending on **low** speed until the mixture is well blended.

11 Using a teaspoon, drop the peanut butter mixture on top of the chocolate mixture in the cake pan.

Swirl it around with a table knife.

12 Place the pan in the oven. Set the timer for 35 to 40 minutes. Test for doneness (see page 10). A toothpick should come out clean. Turn the oven off.

13 Wearing the oven mitts, transfer the cake pan to the cooling rack. If you plan to add an icing or topping to the brownies, cool the cake in the refrigerator first.

Fudge Icing

INGREDIENTS

1/4 cup evaporated milk
2 tablespoons butter
1 cup firmly packed brown sugar
1 tablespoon corn syrup
1-1/4 cups powdered sugar

UTENSILS

Measuring cups and spoons •
Small saucepan • Wooden spoon
• Wire cooling rack
• Electric mixer • Spatula

1 Put the milk, butter, and brown sugar in the small saucepan. Turn the stove on to **medium** heat and place the saucepan on the stove.

2 Stir carefully with the wooden spoon until the mixture bubbles (boils). Boil for 3 minutes. Turn the heat off.

3 Transfer the saucepan to the wire cooling rack.

4 Using the electric mixer on **medium-high** speed, add the corn syrup to the saucepan and beat until creamy and smooth.

5 Add the powdered sugar (1/4 cup at a time) and continue beating until smooth. Stop to scrape the sides of the bowl with the spatula.

6 Spread the icing on the cooled cake.

Peanut/Chocolate Icing

INGREDIENTS

1 tablespoon butter
4 squares (4 ounces)
  unsweetened chocolate
1 cup butterscotch chips
1 cup peanut butter
1 cup shelled roasted peanuts

UTENSILS

Measuring cups and spoons •
Medium saucepan
• Wooden spoon • Spatula

1 Put the butter in the saucepan. Turn the stove on to **low** and place the saucepan on the stove. Stir with the wooden spoon until the butter melts.

2 Immediately add the chocolate squares, butterscotch chips, and peanut butter. Stir with the wooden spoon to form a smooth paste.

3 Add the peanuts and stir to mix. Turn the heat off.

4 Spread the mixture over the cooled brownies. Chill in the refrigerator to set.

Allow the brownies to stand at room temperature for 5 minutes before cutting into squares.

79

PB Icing

INGREDIENTS

1/4 cup (1/2 stick) butter, at room temperature
1/4 cup peanut butter
1 teaspoon vanilla extract
1-1/2 cups powdered sugar
3 tablespoons milk

UTENSILS

**Measuring cups and spoons •
Small mixing bowl
• Electric mixer • Spatula**

1 Put the butter, the peanut butter, and vanilla in a small mixing bowl. Using the electric mixer on **low** speed, beat to blend the ingredients.

2 Add the powdered sugar, a little at a time, beating until the mixture is smooth.

Stop from time to time to scrape the sides of the bowl with the spatula.

3 Add the milk. Beat until creamy.

4 Spread the icing on the brownies. Place in the refrigerator to cool. Cut into squares.

Butterscotch Beasties

Makes 12 beasties

INGREDIENTS

3 tablespoons plus 1 teaspoon
    butter, at room temperature
2-1/2 cups mini-marshmallows
3 cups chow mein noodles
3/4 cup butterscotch chips
2 tablespoons cold water
1/4 cup peanut butter

UTENSILS

Cookie sheet • Wax paper
• Measuring cups and spoons •
Large saucepan • Wooden spoon
• Wire cooling rack • Fork
• Microwave-safe mixing bowl
• Oven mitts

1 Line the cookie sheet with wax paper.

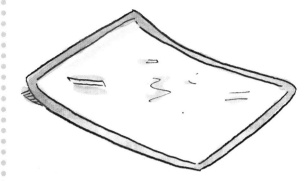

2 Place the 3 tablespoons of butter and the marshmallows in the large saucepan. Turn the stove on to **low** heat and place the saucepan on the stove. Stir with the wooden spoon until the mixture is melted and smooth. Turn the heat off.

3 Transfer the saucepan to the cooling rack. Add the noodles and toss with a fork until coated.

4 Drop spoonfuls of the noodle mixture onto the cookie sheet.

81

5 Put the butterscotch chips and 1 teaspoon of butter in the mixing bowl. Microwave for 1 minute and 40 seconds on **medium** power.

6 Remove from the microwave and add water and peanut butter. Stir until smooth.

If sauce is too thick to drizzle, add more water (1 teaspoon at a time).

82

7 Drizzle the butterscotch mixture over the beasties. Place in the refrigerator to harden.

Did you know? When you eat something sticky, be sure to brush your teeth afterwards. If this is not possible, take a drink of water. This will rinse your mouth and the fluoride in the water will help protect your teeth. Bacteria in the mouth change sugar to acid and this attacks tooth enamel to cause cavities.

Sweet Marie Chocolate Treats

Makes 36 treats

INGREDIENTS

4 teaspoons plus 1 teaspoon butter, at room temperature
1/2 cup peanut butter
1/2 cup firmly packed brown sugar
1/2 cup corn syrup
2 cups rice crispies
3/4 cup shelled roasted peanuts
— ICING —
1/2 cup (1 stick) butter
1/4 cup plus 2 tablespoons unsweetened cocoa powder
1/2 cup powdered sugar

UTENSILS

Measuring cups and spoons •
Paper towel • 8″ square cake pan
• Large saucepan • Wooden spoon
• Wire cooling rack • Spatula

1 Using the paper towel, spread 1 teaspoon of butter evenly over the bottom and sides of the cake pan.

2 Put the peanut butter, brown sugar, corn syrup, and 4 teaspoons of butter in the saucepan. Turn the stove on to **low** heat and place the saucepan on the stove.

Stir the mixture with the wooden spoon until it is melted and smooth. Turn the heat off.

3 Transfer the saucepan to the cooling rack. **Quickly** add the cereal and peanuts to the peanut butter mixture. Stir with the wooden spoon to coat the cereal.

4 Spread the mixture evenly over the bottom of the cake pan, using your fingertips and the spatula.

5 Place in the refrigerator to harden. Clean the saucepan.

6 To make the icing, put the 1/2 cup of butter in the saucepan. Turn the stove on to **low** heat and place the saucepan on the stove. Stir with the wooden spoon until melted.

7 Add the cocoa and the powdered sugar, and stir until melted and smooth. Turn the heat off. Transfer the saucepan to the cooling rack.

83

8 Pour the icing evenly over the cereal mixture, spreading it with the spatula.

9 Place in the refrigerator to harden. When ready, cut into squares and serve.

Did you know?
You can prevent an accident by turning the handle of a saucepan inward when it is on the stove. This positions the saucepan so that it cannot be reached by young children, or knocked off the stove by someone who could bump it.

Made-in-the-Pan Chocolate Cake with PB Icing

Makes 24 pieces

INGREDIENTS

1-1/2 cups sifted flour
1 cup sugar
1/4 cup unsweetened cocoa powder
1 teaspoon baking soda
1/2 teaspoon salt
6 tablespoons oil
1 tablespoon vinegar
1 teaspoon vanilla extract
1 cup cold water
PB Icing (page 80)

UTENSILS

Measuring cups and spoons •
Sifter • 8" square cake pan
• Medium mixing bowl
• Spatula • Fork • Oven mitts
• Wire cooling rack

1 Place the oven rack near the center of the oven. Turn on the oven to 350°F.

2 Sift the flour into the bowl. Measure 1-1/2 cups.

3 Sift the flour again with the sugar, cocoa powder, baking soda, and salt into the **ungreased** cake pan.

4 Stir and spread out the mixture with the spatula, then make 3 holes in the dry ingredients.

5 In 1 hole pour the oil, in 1 hole pour the vinegar, and in 1 hole pour the vanilla.

6 Cover each hole with a third of the water. Stir the mixture with the fork until well blended.

7 Place the pan in the oven. Set the timer for 25 to 30 minutes. Test for doneness. The toothpick should come out clean (see page 10).

Turn the oven off. Wearing the oven mitts, transfer the cake to the cooling rack. Cool completely. Ice with PB Icing.

PB Chocolate Pieces

Makes 36 pieces

INGREDIENTS

1 cup (2 sticks) plus 1 tablespoon
butter, at room temperature
1-3/4 cups graham cracker crumbs
1 cup peanut butter
2-1/2 cups powdered sugar
— TOPPING —
1/2 cup peanut butter
12 ounces semi-sweet chocolate
chips

UTENSILS

Measuring cups and spoons •
13"x 9" cake pan • Paper towel
•1 large, 1 small saucepan
• Wooden spoon
• Wire cooling rack

1 Using the paper towel, spread 1 tablespoon of butter evenly over the bottom and sides of the cake pan.

2 Put 1 cup of butter in the saucepan. Turn the stove on to **medium** heat and place the saucepan on the stove. Stir the mixture with the wooden spoon until the butter is melted. Turn off the heat. Transfer the saucepan to the cooling rack.

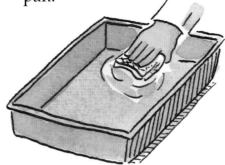

3 Add the graham cracker crumbs, the peanut butter, and powdered sugar to the melted butter. Mix well with the wooden spoon.

4 Press into the cake pan with the spoon and your hand. Place in the refrigerator to harden.

5 Put the topping ingredients in the small saucepan. Turn the stove on to **medium** heat and place the saucepan on the stove. Stir with the wooden spoon until the mixture is melted.

6 Pour the topping over the crust. Place in the refrigerator to harden. Cut into squares.

86

Vanilla PB Squares

Makes 16 squares

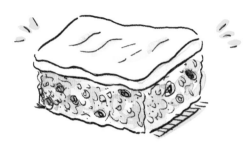

INGREDIENTS

1/4 cup (1/2 stick) plus 1 teaspoon
    butter, at room temperature
1/4 cup peanut butter
1/2 cup sugar
24 vanilla wafers
1/2 cup shelled roasted peanuts
1 teaspoon vanilla extract
1/2 cup raisins

UTENSILS

Measuring cups and spoons •
Paper towel • 8" square cake pan
• Large saucepan • Wooden spoon
• Wire cooling rack • Wax paper
• Rolling pin • Spatula

1 Using the paper towel, spread 1 teaspoon of butter evenly over the bottom and sides of the cake pan.

2 Put 1/4 cup of butter, the peanut butter, and sugar in the saucepan. Turn the stove on to **medium** heat and place the saucepan on the stove.

3 Stir with the wooden spoon until the mixture bubbles (boils). Boil for 1 minute, **stirring constantly**. Turn the heat off.

4 Transfer the saucepan to the cooling rack.

5 Put the wafers between 2 sheets of wax paper. Roll with the rolling pin to crush the wafers.

6 Crush the peanuts in the same way as the wafers (**Step 5**).

7 Add the vanilla, crushed wafers, crushed peanuts, and raisins to the peanut butter mixture in the saucepan. Stir until well mixed.

8 Press the mixture evenly into the cake pan with your fingertips or a spoon.

9 Ice with PB Icing (see page 80). Place the iced cake in the refrigerator to set. When the icing is firm, cut into squares and serve.

Did you know?
Peanuts are used to make peanut butter, lipstick, axle grease, linoleum, and many other products. Peanuts are the most important oil-bearing seed in the world.

No-bake PB Cheesecake

Makes 25 pieces

INGREDIENTS

1/3 cup (5-1/3 tablespoons) butter
1-1/3 cups chocolate cookie crumbs
1/4 cup sugar
4 (3-ounce) packages cream cheese
1/2 cup peanut butter
2 teaspoons vanilla extract
1/2 cup powdered sugar
1 container (16 ounces) frozen
    whipped topping, thawed
1 cup chocolate chips
1/4 cup Chocolate PB Sauce (page 60)
1/2 cup shelled roasted peanuts

UTENSILS

Measuring cups and spoons •
Microwave-safe cup • Wooden
spoon • 1 small, 1 large mixing bowl
• 9" springform pan
• Electric mixer • Spatula
• Wax paper • Rolling pin

1 Put the butter in the microwave-safe cup and heat on **medium** power for 10 seconds.

2 Put the chocolate cookie crumbs, melted butter, and sugar in the small mixing bowl. Stir the ingredients with the wooden spoon.

3 Press the crumb mixture evenly on the bottom and 2 inches up the sides of the springform pan using your fingertips or a spoon.

4 Put the cream cheese, peanut butter, vanilla, and powdered sugar in the large mixing bowl. Using the electric mixer on **medium** speed, beat until the mixture looks light and creamy.

5 Add the frozen whipped topping and chocolate chips. Stir with the wooden spoon until blended.

6 Using the spatula, spread the mixture over the crust in the pan.

7 Spread the Chocolate PB Sauce over the top of the cheesecake.

8 Place the peanuts between 2 sheets of wax paper. Roll with the rolling pin to crush them.

Sprinkle the crushed peanuts on top of the cheesecake. Freeze before serving.

This cheesecake will keep in the freezer for up to 6 weeks.

Tips—Wrap all freezer items well for storing to prevent freezer burn.

PB Dessert Pizza

Makes 10 servings

INGREDIENTS

— CRUST —
3 tablespoons powdered sugar
1/2 cup (1 stick) butter, melted
2 tablespoons peanut butter
1-1/4 cups flour
1/3 cup firmly packed brown sugar
— TOPPING —
4 (3-ounce) packages cream cheese
2 tablespoons peanut butter
1/2 cup sugar
1 teaspoon vanilla extract
Variety of fresh or canned fruit

UTENSILS

Measuring cups and spoons •
1 large, 1 small mixing bowl • Fork
• 12" pizza pan • Oven mitts
• Wire cooling rack • Electric mixer
• Spatula • Bread board
• Paring knife • Sieve

1 Place the oven rack near the center of the oven. Turn on the oven to 350°F.

2 Put all the crust ingredients in the large mixing bowl. Stir with a fork until the dough forms a ball.

3 Place the ball in the center of the **ungreased** pizza pan. Press the dough down with your fingertips and the palms of your hands.

The pizza crust should cover the bottom and sides of the pan evenly.

4 Place the pan in the oven and set the timer for 10 to 15 minutes. Bake until golden brown. Turn the oven off.

5 Wearing the oven mitts, transfer the pizza pan to the cooling rack. Cool 5 minutes.

Place in the refrigerator to cool completely.

6 Make the topping. Put the cream cheese, peanut butter, sugar, and vanilla in the small mixing bowl. Using the electric mixer on **low** speed, beat the mixture until it is smooth and creamy.

7 Spread the topping over the cooled crust.

8 Wash and dry the fruit you have chosen. Using the breadboard and paring knife, cut the fruit into bite-size pieces. Or drain canned mixed fruit.

9 Arrange the fruit in a pattern on the pizza crust. Place in the refrigerator until firm.

> **Tips**—Make the pizza the same day you are serving it.
>
> When using fresh fruit, oranges and bananas should be peeled. Leave the skin on apples, pears, and peaches.
>
> *To prevent the fruit from turning brown*—Make a fruit glaze. Put 1/4 cup apricot jam or orange marmalade into a sieve over a small bowl. Add 1 tablespoon of water. Stir and press the liquid into the small bowl. Drip over the fruit on the pizza. Allow to set.

PB Honey Pie

Makes 1 pie

INGREDIENTS

4 eggs
3/4 cup honey
1/2 cup peanut butter
1/4 cup (1/2 stick) butter, at room temperature
1/2 teaspoon vanilla extract
1 cup shelled roasted peanuts
1/2 cup sesame seeds
1 unbaked pie shell (if frozen, thaw)
Whipped topping or
   Cream Cheese Icing (page 18)

UTENSILS

Measuring cups and spoons •
1 large, 1 small mixing bowl
• Electric mixer • Spatula
• Wax paper • Rolling pin
• Oven mitts
• Wire cooling rack

1 Place the oven rack near the center of the oven. Turn on the oven to 350°F.

2 Break the eggs into the mixing bowl. Using the electric mixer at **medium** speed, beat until the eggs are frothy.

3 Add the honey, peanut butter, butter, and vanilla and beat until blended. Stop the mixer from time to time to scrape the sides of the bowl with the spatula.

4 Put the peanuts between 2 sheets of wax paper. Roll with the rolling pin to crush.

5 Add the crushed peanuts and sesame seeds to the egg mixture. Stir with the spatula to blend.

6 Pour into the pie shell and place in the oven. Set the timer for 45 to 55 minutes.

The pie is done when a toothpick inserted in the center comes out clean (no batter on it).

7 Turn the oven off. Wearing the oven mitts, transfer the pie to the cooling rack.

8 Serve the pie warm with whipped topping or cold with Cream Cheese Icing.

PB Fudge

Makes 36 pieces

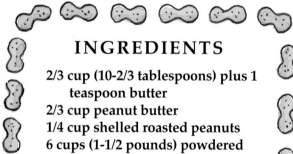

INGREDIENTS

2/3 cup (10-2/3 tablespoons) plus 1 teaspoon butter

2/3 cup peanut butter

1/4 cup shelled roasted peanuts

6 cups (1-1/2 pounds) powdered sugar

1/3 cup milk

1 tablespoon vanilla extract

UTENSILS

Measuring cups and spoons • Paper towel • 9" square cake pan • Large microwave-safe mixing bowl • Oven mitts • Wooden spoon • Wax paper • Rolling pin • Spatula • Plastic wrap

1 Using the paper towel, spread 1 teaspoon of butter evenly over the bottom and sides of the cake pan.

2 Put the 2/3 cup of butter and the peanut butter in the mixing bowl. Place it in the microwave on **high** power for 1-1/2 to 2 minutes.

3 Wearing the oven mitts, remove the bowl from the microwave and stir the mixture with the wooden spoon to blend.

4 Place the peanuts between 2 sheets of wax paper and roll with the rolling pin to crush.

5 Add the crushed peanuts, powdered sugar, milk, and vanilla to the melted peanut butter mixture. Stir until the lumps of sugar disappear.

6 Place the bowl in the microwave again and microwave for 1 to 1-1/2 minutes on **high** power until the mixture is blended, **but not bubbling**.

7 Remove from the microwave and stir until smooth.

8 Pour the fudge into the cake pan, using the spatula to scrape the bowl. Put plastic wrap over the pan to cover it. Place the pan in the refrigerator for 1 hour or more. Cut fudge into small pieces.

MEASUREMENT CONVERSION TABLE	
U.S. measure	Standard metric measure
SPOONS	
1/4 teaspoon	1 milliliter (ml)
1/2 teaspoon	2 ml
1 teaspoon	5 ml
2 teaspoons	10 ml
1 tablespoon (T)	15 ml
CUPS	
1/4 cup (4 T)	50 ml
1/3 cup (5-1/3 T)	75 ml
1/2 cup (8 T)	125 ml
2/3 cup (10-2/3 T)	150 ml
3/4 cup (12 T)	175 ml
1 cup (16 T)	250 ml
4-1/2 cups	1 (L) litre
WEIGHTS	
1 ounce (oz)	30 grams (g)
2 oz	55 g
3 oz	85 g
4 oz	125 g
5 oz	140 g
6 oz	170 g
7 oz	200 g
8 oz	500 g
16 oz (1 pound)	1000 g
32 oz (2 pounds)	1 kilogram (kg)

OVEN TEMPERATURES

150°F	65°C	375°F	190°C
250°F	120°C	400°F	200°C
325°F	160°C	425°F	210°C
350°F	180°C		

baking preparations, 9
bananas
  pb-banana bread, 52
  pb-banana cookies, 69
  pb-banana milkshake, 12
  pb-banana roll-ups, 20
breads
  pb-banana bread, 52
brownies
  pb brownies, 76

cake
  made-in-the-pan chocolate cake, 84
candy
  pb chocolate pieces, 86
  pb fudge, 94
carrots
  carrot wagon wheels, 67
  how to shred, 68
  pb spicy chicken and noodles, 36
cereals
  cereal snack, 15
  grandpa's hearty cookies, 71
  granola bars, 16
  pb-granola, 19
  sweet marie chocolate treats, 82
cheese, 5
  cream cheese icing, 18
  easy-as-pie pizza, 39
  no-bake pb cheesecake, 89
  pb dessert pizza 91
  pb honey pie, 92
  peanutty nachos, 38
  Thai chicken pizza, 42
  toasty pb melt, 30
cheesecake
  no-bake pb cheesecake, 89
chicken
  chicken stir-fry, 45
  quick pb soup, 28
  Thai chicken pizza, 42

chocolate
  chocolate pb sauce, 60
  fudge icing, 78
  made-in-the-pan chocolate cake, 84
  pb brownies, 76
  pb-chocolate milkshake, 12
  pb-chocolate pieces, 86
  peanut/chocolate icing, 79
  peanutty hot chocolate, 13
  sweet marie chocolate treats, 82
cookies
  carrot wagon wheels, 67
  grandpa's hearty cookies, 71
  lollipop cookies, 66
  pb-banana cookies, 69
  pb cookiegram, 73
  pb hockey puck sandwiches, 63
  pb pinwheels, 61
  traditional pb cookies, 65
crusts, 21
  easy-as-pie pizza, 39
  pb dessert pizza, 91

dips
  pb dip, 29
doneness test, 10
dough
  modeling, 70
dressings
  pb dressing, 34
  spicy dressing, 36
drinks
  pb-banana milkshake, 12
  pb-chocolate milkshake, 12
  peanutty hot chocolate, 13

eggs, 5
  how to crack, 10

food guide, 4
fruit glaze, 92
fruits
  ants on a log and pb flowers, 14
  fruit roll-ups, 23
  glaze, 92
  orange salad, 34
  pb-banana bread, 52
  pb-banana cookies, 69
  pb-banana milkshake, 12
  pb-banana roll-ups, 20
  pb berry cone, 59
  pb dessert pizza, 91
granola, 19
granola bars, 16

ice cream, 5, 58
  pb-banana milkshake, 12
  pb-chocolate milkshake, 12
  pb berry cone, 59
  pb ice-cream sundae rings, 57
icings
  cream cheese icing, 18
  fudge icing, 78
  peanut/chocolate icing, 79
  pb icing, 80

lunch box tips, 51

main dishes, 4
  chicken stir-fry, 45
  peanutty nachos, 38
  pb fingers, 32
  Thai chicken pizza, 42
  toasty pb melt, 30
measuring
  dry ingredients, 10
  liquid ingredients, 10
measurement conversion table, 95
meats, 4
muffins
  baking tips, 50

meal-in-a-muffin, 51
  pb bran fake muffins, 49
nachos
  peanutty nachos, 38
noodles
  pb butterscotch beasties, 81
  pb spicy chicken and noodles, 36
  with pb sauce, 47

PB, 9
peanut butter
  abbreviation, 9
  fat content, 5
  make your own, 8
  provides nutrients, 4, 46
  smooth or chunky, 7, 8
  space food sticks, 5
  toothache remedy, 6
peanut farmer, 5
peanut names, 5
peanut paste, 6
peanut plant, 5
peanut vendor, 7
peanuts
  as clothing, 53
  as food, 6
  as health food, 6
  as snacks, 6, 7
  at baseball games, 6
  at circuses, 6
  how to grow, 8
  leading food crop, 7
  production, 6
  products, 7, 88
  research, 7
  roasted in the shell, 6
  shelled, roasted, salted, 7
  versatility, 7
peanutty nachos, 38
pies
  pb honey pie, 92
pita pocket, 22
pizza
  easy-as-pie pizza, 39
  pb dessert pizza, 91

Thai chicken pizza, 42
popcorn
  pb caramel corn, 55
raisins
  ants on a log and pb flowers, 14
  grandpa's hearty cookies, 71
  vanilla pb squares, 87
rice
  chicken stir-fry, 45

salads
  orange salad, 34
  pb spicy chicken and noodles, 36
sandwiches
  balanced meal, 26
  basic pb sandwich, 26
  "breadless" sandwich, 27
  fancy pb sandwich, 27
  pb-banana roll-ups, 20
  pb sandwich variations, 27
  pita pocket, 22
  toasty pb melt, 30
sauces
  chocolate pb sauce, 60
  pb sauce, 47
setting the table, 24
spreads
  pb spread, 29
soups
  quick pb soup, 28
squares
  pb brownies, 76
  sweet marie chocolate treats, 82
  vanilla pb squares, 87

vegetables, 4
  chicken stir-fry, 45
  dips, 29
  orange salad, 34
  pb spicy chicken and noodles, 36
  with pb sauce, 47